Portfolio Assessment

Uses, Cases, Scoring, and Impact

Edited by Trudy W. Banta

Assessment
UPdate
C O L L E C T I O N S

Published by Jossey-Bass
A Wiley Imprint
989 Market Street, San Francisco, CA 94103-1741   www.josseybass.com

Jossey-Bass books and products are available through most bookstores. To contact Jossey-Bass directly call our Customer Care Department within the U.S. at 800-956-7739, outside the U.S. at 317-572-3986, or fax 317-572-4002.

Jossey-Bass also publishes its books in a variety of electronic formats. Some content that appears in print may not be available in electronic books.

Library of Congress Cataloging-in-Publication Data

Portfolio assessment: an assessment update collection/edited by Trudy W. Banta.—1st ed.
    p. cm.
  Includes bibliographical references.
  ISBN 0-7879-7286-X (alk. paper)
  1. Portfolios in education. 2. Educational tests and measurements. I. Banta, Trudy W.
LB1029.P67P657 2003
378.1'664—dc22

                                                  2003024183

Contents

How Can Portfolios Be Scored?

How Can We Judge the Impact and the Validity of Portfolios?

Introduction: Why Portfolios?

Trudy W. Banta

In recent years there has been a virtual explosion of interest in portfolios. Why? A review of literature on portfolios that appeared in issue number 6:4 of *Assessment Update* by Janet E. Boyle sums up the appeal of this assessment approach:

> The portfolio, as an element of authentic assessment, has captured the interest of many instructors who want a more comprehensive way to assess their students' knowledge and skills, to have students actively participate in the evaluation process, and to simultaneously develop students' skills of reflective thinking. These latter features make portfolios an attractive alternative to traditional summative testing (p. 10).

In her review Janet Boyle points to five key characteristics of portfolios (see italicized phrases below) that make this approach to assessing college student learning so important that I have chosen it as the subject of this special collection of articles from *Assessment Update*.

Faculty are hungry for *alternatives to traditional summative testing* that will provide more *comprehensive ways to assess students' knowledge and skills*. They recognize that no single instrument can measure all that students know about a concept or issue, that not every student will be up to giving their best performance on any specific occasion, and that the important element of growth over time cannot be assessed with a single measurement. Thus faculty seek *authentic assessment* of the range of students' knowledge and skills. Portfolios can yield this assessment as students demonstrate what they know and can do, as well as their diverse talents and learning styles, using a variety of artifacts and media in collections of their own work over the period of a semester, a year or two, or an entire college career.

Another characteristic of traditional summative assessment that troubles faculty and students alike is that too often it is developed by faculty and administered to students without their involvement—involvement that could deepen and strengthen student understanding. Using portfolios, *students actively participate in the evaluation process*, selecting materials to include and combine as evidence of specific learnings. Many students take portfolio development very seriously because they plan to use some of the contents to convince potential employers that they have unique skills and talents. And because an essential feature of preparing a portfolio is reflecting on the content and explaining how components fit together to illustrate what has been learned, portfolios *simultaneously develop students' skills of reflective thinking*.

Just how popular are student portfolios as assessment tools? For many years faculty in English and fine arts have used portfolios to evaluate student progress and achievement. In the early 1970s faculty at Alverno and Manhattanville Colleges began to assess a much wider range of competences via portfolios. By the late 1980s, portfolios were being used in assessing the effectiveness of general education. In 1999 I conducted an informal but systematic content analysis of the program for the annual Assessment Conference sponsored by the American Association for Higher Education and reported in my *Editor's Notes* column that "about 40 percent of the sessions that focused on methods dealt with the use of portfolios" (*Assessment Update*, 1999, Vol. 11, No. 5, p. 3). Noting the growing interest in electronic portfolios, I went on to say that "nearly 40 percent of the portfolio sessions were about electronic portfolios." On the basis of this evidence, I was willing to assert even as early as that article in 1999 that ". . . portfolios, particularly those that use Web-based technology, have great appeal for many faculty and are becoming the instrument of choice for assessment on a growing number of campuses." While I have not seen usage statistics since then, my experience indicates that portfolio use on campuses has grown exponentially in the intervening years.

Portfolios' Strengths and Challenges

Like any other approach to assessment, portfolios have drawbacks as well as strengths. Above all, they require time. It stands to reason that an assessment method which is comprehensive, and permits a look not just at a student's current levels of knowledge and skill but also at the ways in which learning has developed over time, would require extra effort to plan and to evaluate. Initially faculty must decide what purposes the portfolio will serve, what kind of information will be included, when the artifacts will be gathered, and how the content will be assessed. Where and how will the portfolios be stored? Even with electronic portfolios, dedicated servers may be needed if thousands of students' work is to be submitted for review. Who will have access to which parts of individual portfolios? With electronic portfolios, expensive programming will be required to establish differential access to materials for students, faculty, employers, and others.

Since portfolios permit the display of authentic evidence of what students know and can do, they have face validity for all concerned; that is, portfolios appear to be credible sources of information about what faculty are teaching and what students are learning. But demonstrating validity using traditional definitions and approaches has proven problematic. Scoring is often holistic and different observers see different things, so inter-rater agreement is often difficult to achieve, particularly in the very large middle range of performance between "outstanding" and "failing." Holistic scores are somewhat subjective and thus harder than more objective measures to interpret and to compare across programs or institutions. As convincing and exciting as it may be for an employer to see and hear about a senior project via an electronic portfolio, he or she may express a preference for a single standardized test score when confronted with senior projects for 50 competing job applicants and no convenient guidelines for comparing them.

Despite the challenges that portfolios present, those who use them prefer them to other methods because they are so versatile and adaptable and accommodate such rich information. Portfolios enable faculty to see firsthand not only *what* students are learning but *how* they are learning. So faculty can gain a deeper understanding of the successes and failures of their teaching strategies and their curricula. Students also learn from the experience of developing a portfolio. As they make selections for inclusion and reflect on what they have learned, they make connections between components of a course and among courses in their curriculum and thus derive new meaning from their educational experiences. Both faculty and students benefit from being able to show employers and other stakeholders details of the process of promoting student learning in college.

In addition to their usefulness in assessing student learning and development over time, portfolios also can play a role in assessing the effectiveness of courses, curricula, and even institutions. Content analysis of individual student portfolios using rubrics designed for that purpose can show faculty general areas of strength and weakness in student performance in a course, in general education, and in the curriculum of an academic major. Illustrative excerpts conveying the range of student work, accompanied by the scoring rubrics faculty have applied to the work, can be used in an institutional portfolio for accreditation or accountability reports. With the addition of data from constituent surveys and other data-gathering methods, a narrative summary of institutional performance can be conveyed to a worldwide audience via an electronic institutional portfolio.

Organization of this Collection

In the almost 15 years of *Assessment Update*'s history, approximately 40 articles about portfolios have appeared. All were published because they had something important to say about the development of this versatile assessment tool. Thus it has been very difficult for us to select a mere baker's dozen for this issue. Ultimately we decided to organize the issue in four sections, each containing three or four illustrative selections. The first section provides an overview, defining terms and tracing some of the history of portfolio use through the literature. Next we present a range of examples of portfolio use in assessment, first in general education, then in the major, and finally in institutional accreditation.

Perhaps the major challenges confronting those who wish to use portfolios relate to evaluating the learning portfolios demonstrate and establishing the credibility of this approach to assessment. These challenges are reflected in the last two sections of this volume, *How Can Portfolios Be Scored?* and *How Can We Judge the Impact and Validity of Portfolios?*

Further Reading

For those interested in further reading about portfolios, the following publications provide additional perspectives:

Electronic Portfolios: Emerging Practices in Student, Faculty, and Institutional Learning. Barbara Cambridge (ed.), Washington, DC: American Association for Higher Education, 2001.

"Portfolio Assessment." Lendley C. Black. In T.W. Banta & Associates, *Making a Difference—Outcomes of a Decade of Assessment in Higher Education*. San Francisco: Jossey-Bass, 1993. (Now available from National Center for Higher Education Management Systems, Boulder, CO.)

Time Will Tell: Portfolio-Assisted Assessment of General Education. Aubrey Forrest. Washington, DC: American Association for Higher Education, 1990.

Truman State University Web Site: http://assessment.truman.edu/Portfolio.htm.

What Is a Portfolio?

Using Portfolios to Assess the Impact of a Curriculum

Richard L. Larson

This article provides an overview of portfolio assessment, examining various ways it can be used and scored, as well as its strengths and potential shortcomings. From Assessment Update 3:2, March-April 1991.

A portfolio, it is important to say at the start, is nothing more complicated than a collection of a person's works: stories, poems, sketches, paintings, advertising designs—or academic writings. Portfolios can include larger or smaller numbers of works. They may or may not be accompanied by a statement, written by the compiler, to introduce items in the portfolio, explain how the compiler decided what to include in the portfolio, or describe how the compiler evaluates his own work.

Portfolios can be planned: the writer or artist knows all along that particular compositions, or a selection of her work, will be going into a portfolio. Or they can be unplanned: the compiler had not decided, when she completed the individual works, that she would bring some of them together to be viewed as a group. Portfolios may be assembled to demonstrate the compiler's specific accomplishments, to reveal the range of the compiler's work, or to include all the work that a person has completed in a particular period of time.

The portfolio may include drafts of writings, as well as finished works, and compiling the portfolio can provide the opportunity to revise, perfect, or polish the items to be included, so that they represent the person's best work at the time the portfolio is compiled. Although simple in basic concept, portfolios can be versatile ways of presenting creative accomplishments.

Let us now suppose that those in charge of assessing the accomplishments of students in a major field, or determining how well the curriculum in the major is educating students in that field, want to find out what students have been learning. Or suppose that those in charge of a program in general education want to find out whether students are mastering the cognitive activities and strategies that the program in general education is expected to teach. One way to learn whether students are developing as the faculty hopes is to examine some of the writings the students have produced within the major or within the courses designed for general education.

The faculty can ask some students, or all, to compile a selection from their writings for submission in a portfolio. The number of writings requested can be few or many. Faculty members can indicate which courses should be represented among the writings in the portfolio and can even stipulate, if they wish, the kinds of writings students should include. The faculty in literature can say that the portfolio must include writings about literary works in different genres, together with writing in which students discuss a common theme in works from many genres. Or the faculty can ask that the portfolio include an interpretation of a poem, a journal entry recording the student's response to a particular character, or a piece showing the student's ability to research critical theory. The faculty supervising the program in general education can request that the portfolios include an evaluation of a book from a field other than that of the student's major, a laboratory report, a proposal for solving a social or political problem, or an interpretation of a work of art. What the faculty requests, if outlined before the student begins the program under review, can influence instruction. Teachers will have the opportunity to require students to write the kinds of pieces that will be put into their portfolios.

How can portfolios be scored to reveal features of the student's work in the major, or the impact of a general education program? That the portfolio contains appropriate pieces from the required mix of courses might be considered sufficient, or a faculty committee can develop a scoring scale, with descriptors for each point on the scale, that will measure characteristics the faculty values in students' work. A possible descriptor for a top score might be "All papers reveal the ability to cite evidence for assertions, to evaluate the cogency of that evidence, and to draw reasonable conclusions from data. The reasoning in all papers can be followed from beginning to end, and all papers reveal sure command of English vocabulary and syntax."

Scores can be summed or averaged to reach a composite, although a group of pieces gathered together for a composite score loses some of the value of a portfolio. Portfolios can be read analytically, with close attention paid to specific kinds of cognitive strategies that students employ to deal with different interpretive problems or different texts. The pieces in the portfolio can also be arranged and read in chronological order, to see whether students are developing the powers of reading, reasoning, and assembling discussions that the faculty is trying to teach.

Recognizable strengths in portfolios may reveal not just the native ability that students have brought to the campus but also the influence of curricula and teaching. Conspicuous shortcomings in, say, reasoning and interpretation of data in several portfolios may point to a need for revising the curriculum, the instruction, the specific writing assignments given, or all three. The faculty must decide which procedures for reading portfolios will provide the needed information, while keeping to a reasonable minimum the cost, in time and dollars, of the readings. One way to keep down costs may be to examine only a judiciously chosen sample of the portfolios submitted.

At Lehman College, under a FIPSE grant designed to evaluate the impact of a recently installed curriculum in general education, we asked students at various levels of progress to give us, voluntarily, portfolios in which each had to contain three pieces of writing, each piece had to be at least three pages long, and no piece could come from English composition courses. We read these portfolios first to identify cognitive and rhetorical activities in their content, such as reviewing and evaluating others' research, reporting an experiment, evaluating a text, interpreting the significance of an event, generalizing about a social condition, or making recommendations to solve a political problem. We read the portfolios again to see how regularly the pieces in each one reflected the abilities we value in writing, such as reasoning sensibly to conclusions, recognizing and qualifying general statements, recognizing assumptions and implications of statements, and selecting organizational plans appropriate to the data examined and to the writer's interpretation of the data.

We record the frequency with which students carry out various cognitive and rhetorical activities and exhibit the qualities we value in their writing. We will report to our faculty at large, as well as to our administration, which of the rhetorical activities students are assigned or encouraged to perform and which they are not, and which of the qualities that we value in writing are found in the portfolios and which are not. From these findings, we will make recommendations for curriculum change or for adjustment of emphases in instruction. We may want to include more writing assignments, require specific cognitive or rhetorical acts in various courses, or give students more practice in locating and interpreting data needed for developing writings. We will almost surely recommend efforts to prepare faculty to offer the instruction students need in order to develop the abilities they seem not to be developing.

Reading texts intently, as our procedure requires, will enable us, we are sure, to discover much about what our students are learning to do, cognitively and rhetorically. Making such discoveries is one way of monitoring the effectiveness of our college's program in general education.

Richard L. Larson is project director of the Project on College Curricula in Composition, Lehman College of the City University of New York.

Portfolio Assessment: Benefits, Issues of Implementation, and Reflections on Its Use

Lorie Cook-Benjamin

For readers interested in documentation of the benefits of portfolio assessment, as well as information on how it has been used, to what effect, and suggestions for implementation, this literature review points the way to a range of resources. From Assessment Update 13:4, July-August 2001.

Portfolio assessment can be defined as a purposeful collection of a student's work that tells a story of the student's efforts, progress, or achievement in one or more areas (Arter and Spandel, 1992). Research suggests that portfolio assessment provides benefits that more traditional measures do not provide.

Benefits of Portfolio Assessment

Henkin (1993) finds that the portfolio provides a holistic assessment that contributes to a valid measure of higher-order thinking skills. According to Calvin (1993), when students are assessed using authentic materials such as portfolios, bias is reduced. Students also profit from the portfolio by becoming better evaluators and practicing self-reflection in their work (Gilman and McDermott, 1994; Lambdin and Walker, 1994; Newman and Smolen, 1993; Snyder, Elliot, Bhavnagri, and Boyer, 1993; Tierney, 1992). Lambdin and Walker (1994) find that students develop better self-assessment skills and become less reliant on grades when portfolio assessment is used.

Cohen (1995) and McClelland (1991) caution against the use of grades as a measure of student achievement. McClelland states that "portfolio evaluation encourages us, even forces us, to focus on text and not on grades" (p. 171). According to Wiggins (1994), "the use of a single grade to represent achievement, progress, and growth leads to the difficulty of grading fairly" (p. 33). Portfolio assessment has been found to provide the teacher with a more holistic assessment than is characteristically used in traditional assessments (Calfee and Perfumo, 1993; Henkin, 1993; Lambdin and Walker, 1994; Newman and Smolen, 1993; Viechnicki and others, 1993). Kieffer and Morrison (1994) report that the portfolio is more authentic in that it involves a gathering of multiple sources of evidence. Another strength of portfolio assessment is reported by Stahle and Mitchell (1993), who find that students and teachers receive the mutual benefit of being able to access student material more easily with a portfolio than without.

Lambdin and Walker (1994) used the portfolio because they "wanted to establish a better means of communication among students, parents, and teachers" (p. 318). According to Calfee and Perfumo (1993) and Lucas-Lescher (1995), the portfolio affords more opportunity for students and teachers to engage in dialogue and maintain communication. Promoting a positive attitude in students and teachers is another strength of portfolios that is noted in the portfolio literature (Perkins and Gelfer, 1993; Ryan and Kuhs, 1993; Stahle and Mitchell, 1993). More specifically, Perkins and Gelfer find that portfolios improve the work attitudes of schoolteachers.

Issues of Portfolio Implementation

Review of the literature also suggests issues that should be considered before implementing a portfolio approach. For instance, deciding how to assess the contents is a major issue to be decided prior to implementing a portfolio assessment system (Adams and Hamm, 1992; Calfee and Perfumo, 1993; Cramer, 1993; Gilman and McDermott, 1994; Valeri-Gold, Olson, and Deming, 1991). Nelson (1995) warns that instructors should not rush into using portfolio assessment until the needs for using the portfolio have been examined. For example, will this portfolio measure replace other assessment methods or supplement them?

In determining the portfolio's purpose, decisions must be made about who will view the portfolio (Cramer, 1993). Will the student, teacher, parents, or potential employers be allowed to read the contents? Who should determine what is in the portfolio—the teacher or the student? Cramer (1993) believes students should have a say about the contents of their portfolios.

Lambdin and Walker (1994) have raised a concern about how the portfolio will be stored. Also, who will be responsible for storing it?

Reflections on My Use of Portfolios

Having used portfolio assessment for over a decade, I have come to several realizations. First, there is no right way to create a portfolio! Yes, there are several issues to consider in creating a portfolio assessment system, but the portfolio must reflect the class or program in which it is used. The second realization is that the portfolio continually evolves. Students change, and new information is gathered that must be reflected in the portfolio assessment system. The final realization pertains to the effect that portfolio assessment has on students. At first students are hesitant and maybe even a little resistant. (After all, for most students the portfolio represents a change in the way they are accustomed to being assessed.) Eventually, however, they come to realize the benefits of the portfolio. In working with students, I have found that they feel a sense of accomplishment in the completeness of the portfolio. They see the growth they have achieved and the areas in which they still need to improve. I have also found that students use the portfolio as a referral device in later classes, an act I have not observed with traditional assessments.

In summary, deciding to create a portfolio assessment system will take time, effort, and the understanding that the portfolio is a "creation." I have found, however, that the benefits of its use far outweigh those offered by traditional assessments.

References

Adams, D. M., and Hamm, M. E. "Portfolio Assessment and Social Studies: Collecting, Selecting, and Reflecting on What Is Significant." *Social Education*, 1992, 56, 103–105.

Arter, J., and Spandel, V. "Using Portfolios of Student Work in Instruction and Assessment." *Educational Measurement: Issues and Practice*, 1992, 11, 36–44.

Calfee, R. C., and Perfumo, P. "Student Portfolios: Opportunities for a Revolution in Assessment." *Journal of Reading,* 1993, *36,* 532–537.

Calvin, L. "A Practitioner's View of Current Issues in Assessment." In D. Else (ed.), *Challenges Facing Student Assessment in the 90s: A Collection of Papers.* Cedar Falls: University of Northern Iowa, 1993.

Cohen, P. "Abolish Grades." *Education Update,* May 1995, *37,* 3.

Cramer, S. R. "Navigating the Assessment Maze with Portfolios." *The Clearing House,* Nov.–Dec. 1993, *67,* 72–74.

Gilman, D. A., and McDermott, M. "Portfolio Collections: An Alternative to Testing." *Contemporary Education,* 1994, *65,* 73–76.

Henkin, R. "Emerging Feminist Themes Found in Graduate Students' Portfolios Written by Women Elementary School Teachers." *Action in Teacher Education,* 1993, *15,* 20–28.

Kieffer, R. D., and Morrison, L. S. "Changing Portfolio Process: One Journey Toward Authentic Assessment." *Language Arts,* 1994, *71,* 411–418.

Lambdin, D. V., and Walker, V. L. "Planning for Classroom Portfolio Assessment." *Arithmetic Teacher,* 1994, *41,* 318–324.

Lucas-Lescher, M. *Portfolios: Assessing Learning in the Primary Grades.* Washington, D.C.: NEA Professional Library, 1995.

McClelland, K. "Portfolio: Solution to a Problem." In P. Belanoff and M. Dickson (eds.), *Portfolios: Process and Product.* Portsmouth, N.H.: Heinemann, 1991.

Nelson, C. "How to Design and Implement Student Portfolios." *Faculty Development,* Spring 1995, *8,* 1–2.

Newman, C., and Smolen, L. "Portfolio Assessment in Our Schools: Implementation, Advantages, and Concerns." *Mid-Western Educational Researcher,* 1993, *6,* 28–32.

Perkins, P. G., and Gelfer, J. I. "Portfolio Assessment of Teachers." *The Clearing House,* Mar.–Apr. 1993, *66,* 235–237.

Ryan, J. M., and Kuhs, T. M. "Assessment of Preservice Teachers and the Use of Portfolios." *Theory into Practice,* 1993, *32,* 75–81.

Snyder, J., Elliot, S., Bhavnagri, N. P., and Boyer, J. "Beyond Assessment: University/School Collaboration on Portfolio Review and the Challenge to Program Improvement." *Action in Teacher Education,* 1993, *15,* 55–60.

Stahle, D. L., and Mitchell, J. P. "Portfolio Assessment in College Methods Courses: Practicing What We Preach." *Journal of Reading,* 1993, *36,* 538–542.

Tierney, R. J. "Setting a New Agenda for Assessment." *Learning,* Sept. 1992, *21,* 61–64.

Valeri-Gold, M., Olson, J. R., and Deming, M. P. "Portfolios: Collaborative Authentic Assessment Opportunities for College Developmental Learners." *Journal of Reading,* 1991, *35,* 298–305.

Viechnicki, K. J., Barbour, N., Shaklee, B., Rohrer, J., and Ambrose, R. "The Impact of Portfolio Assessment on Teacher Classroom Activities." *Journal of Teacher Education*, 1993, *44*, 371–377.

Wiggins, G. "Toward Better Report Cards." *Educational Leadership*, 1994, *52*, 28–37.

Lorie Cook-Benjamin is assistant professor of teacher education at Midland Lutheran College.

Electronic Portfolios

Ephraim Schechter, Alec Testa, Douglas Eder

This selection from the Web Corner department of Assessment Update outlines the elements of a good electronic portfolio, describing and offering examples of institutional, faculty, and student portfolios. From Assessment Update 13:4, July-August, 2001.

Electronic portfolios are dispensed on the Web in many flavors, depending on the purposes that give them life and the audiences they aim to serve. One simple classification of e-folios is to use the categories institutional, faculty, and student. Principles of good portfolio construction have existed since the time of guilds during the Middle Ages in Europe, and they endure today in the Web-based virtual environment: (1) show goals, intents, and plans; (2) display work and examples of progress toward goals; (3) provide evidence of accumulating feedback and subsequent reflection; (4) reveal a trail of growth and improvement based on that feedback in order to elevate goals, intents, and plans for the next cycle. A good portfolio communicates these four things clearly to its audience. Accordingly, good Web-based portfolios conform to expectations of good "netiquette" in such properties as page and image size, speed of loading, and breadth of menu choices and hyperlinks.

A collection of *institutional portfolios* as living documents and works in progress can be found through the Urban Universities Portfolio Project

<http://www.imir.iupui.edu/portfolio>. The purpose of the project is to "develop a new medium [and construct] institutional portfolios that demonstrate the universities' effectiveness to various groups of stakeholders." Six universities are developing individual institutional portfolios that, in the context of assessment and reflection about learning, reveal what they are about. As a group, the portfolios reveal institutional goals, visions, and intents. Through accompanying snapshots of demographics, structures, national benchmarks, and finances, they describe "who we are" at present. Under development are those pieces of evidence, such as authentic work, stories, analyses, and the reflective voices of students and faculty, that reveal real institutional effectiveness.

Faculty portfolios abound on the Web and, in general, are found in two main categories. A *course portfolio* generally asks a question about the delivery of a course and acts as written memory of what happened. In contrast, a *teaching portfolio* is a document that usually provides evidence in support of a promotion, merit, or tenure decision. Naturally, they both can be constructed for purely personal reasons. A key element is the reflective voice of the author, either examining evidence to answer a question or assembling evidence in support of a case. A portfolio becomes scholarly when it becomes visible and subject to peer review.

The University of Nebraska–Lincoln displays several course portfolios on its Peer Review of Teaching Web site at <http://www.unl.edu/peerrev/>. The dominant format is the one suggested in *Scholarship Assessed* by Glassik, Huber, and Maeroff (1997). Examples are available. The Teaching Portfolio Project of the American Historical Association/ American Association for Higher Education/Carnegie Foundation, accessible at <http://www.theaha.org/teaching/aahe/aahecover.html>, is another course portfolio site. A key to appreciating the course portfolio is the reflective, analytical question that asks, "What is the influence of different pedagogies on student learning?" So many excellent teaching portfolios exist that it would be unfair to select only a couple as examples. Rather, the two portfolios listed below were selected because of the theme they represent. Barbara Millis identified them as "highly recommended cooperative learning sites" for her Teaching, Learning, and Technology Roundtable Webcast on March 13, 2001 <http://www.tltgroup.org/calendar/millis3–13–01.htm>. The first one, located at <http://www.capecod.net/~tpanitz/tedspage/>, is informal and serves as a window into the personal teaching style of a professor. The second, found at <http://www2.ncsu.edu/unity/lockers/users/f/felder/public/RMF.html>, is equally instructive but is more formal. Both portfolios display research, teaching and learning and service philosophies, techniques, and activities, and do so around the cooperative learning theme. They effectively offer evidence on how their authors see, use, and develop cooperative learning. They bring the scholarship of teaching to the Web.

Student portfolios exist worldwide and as a rule are kept behind password protection for privacy. They vary hugely in purpose, style, and quality. Few generalizations hold. Student portfolios representing disciplines such as architecture or constructed for use in a career development center tend to conform to a conservative style and make a case for eventual employment. Those arising from a college requirement to show intellectual growth often contain samples of writing, video clips of oral presentations, and reflective statements about what has been learned. Portfolios built for a specific course may offer a project, statement, set of references, or designs—any of which might be augmented by images and sound.

In the United States, Kalamazoo College helped lead the experiment with on-line student portfolios, and that college maintains a public resource containing instructions and examples at <http://www.kzoo.edu/pfolio>. Its extensive list of links to other colleges and universities that use on-line portfolios has been transferred to the American Association of Higher Education (AAHE) at <http://www.aahe.org/teaching/pfoliosearch3.cfm>.

Electronic portfolios are the subject of a AAHE publication entitled *Electronic Portfolios: Emerging Practices in Student, Faculty, and Institutional Learning,* Barbara Cambridge, Executive Editor. The Web site for further information is <http://www.aahe.org/teaching/portfolio_projects.htm>.

Compiled by Douglas Eder (e-mail: <deder@siue.edu>) at Southern Illinois University Edwardsville <http://www.siue. edu/~deder/assess/index.html>, Ephraim Schechter (e-mail: <ephraim_schechter@ncsu.edu>) at North Carolina State University, <http://www2.acs.ncsu.edu/UPA/assmt/>, and Alec Testa (e-mail: <atesta@wgu. edu>) at Western Governors' University <http://www.wgu.edu/wgu/academics/ understanding.html>.

How Are Portfolios Being Used?

Electronic Portfolios and the Assessment of Student Learning

Gloria M. Rogers, Timothy Chow

To anyone who has followed closely the development of portfolio assessment, the electronic portfolio developed by Rose-Hulman Institute of Technology will likely be familiar. This article details the thinking that went into the portfolio's design and how it is used, and provides readers with general guidelines on designing a portfolio system for their campuses. From Assessment Update 12:2, January-February 2000.

The goal for student outcomes at Rose-Hulman Institute of Technology is to instill in our graduates the skills appropriate to their profession and to lifelong learning. These skills are further delineated by nine subgoals: ethics, teaming, communication, global awareness, experiments, design, professional practice, interpreting data, and contemporary issues. Each of the nine skills has multiple, measurable, specific performance criteria that define the skill. Faculty researched various data collection methods, including course grades, questionnaires and surveys, standardized tests, qualitative methods, and portfolios. Criteria were developed for selecting a primary data-collection method. First, the method should be rich, offering quality information about students in a broad range of outcome areas. Data collection should produce valid results, reflect the uniqueness of the institution, and be minimally intrusive on the time of students and faculty. Finally, any method used should serve students by engaging them in reflection on their own education and helping them prepare for a career or further education.

After reviewing various data-collection methods, it was determined that portfolios met most of these criteria. Rose-Hulman faculty adopted the portfolio as the primary source of data for assessing student outcomes and evaluating program effectiveness.

RosE-Portfolio Design

The RosE-Portfolio was developed by faculty, staff, and students using the following design requirements:

- Ease of use
- Student-controlled access (rather than access controlled by faculty raters and advisers)
- Ability to archive student materials in multimedia format
- User access via multiple search criteria
- Student ability to update and replace materials
- User access online anytime
- Faculty ability to rate student portfolios online anytime
- Faculty ratings automatically logged and aggregated
- Faculty rater ability to provide students with feedback online
- Student submissions focused on Institute-defined learning outcomes
- File format commonly accessible
- Ability to link curriculum to learning objectives

Once the design specifications were identified, a prototype was developed for evaluation.

The RosE-Portfolio is a Web-based system that allows students to access their portfolios using a local area network user name and password.

An Oracle database server is currently being used. It provides all the archive and search functions necessary to meet the design specifications. The design includes a compression feature that automatically compresses documents when students submit them in the RosE-Portfolio. This helps minimize data storage space needs. We are considering providing each student with his or her electronic portfolio on CD-ROM upon graduation.

In addition to features identified for student use, special views have been developed for faculty raters and faculty advisers. They can search using multiple criteria designed to satisfy their need for quick information retrieval. Faculty raters can search according to learning outcome goals and performance criteria. For those rating a submission, the identity of the student is hidden; rather than the student's name, a system-generated identification number is used. This enables faculty raters to be more objective in assessing student submissions. Faculty advisers have access to the work of their advisees only. They can search submissions by learning outcome goal for all advisees or on any subset of performance criteria, as well as review the entire portfolio for any given advisee. For example, a faculty adviser could perform a search by date of submission to determine whether or not an advisee is keeping her RosE-Portfolio current.

Motivation for Participation

The design of the system provides opportunities for students to customize their RosE-Portfolios. They can present evidence of a variety of skills and knowledge as they seek internships, co-ops, or employment after graduation. The Office of Career Services has been involved in the development of the RosE-Portfolio and anticipates that it will increasingly become a tool students use to present themselves to recruiters. Within their RosE-Portfolio, students are encouraged to build a dynamic résumé, to which they can "hot link" the best of their work in their portfolio. Thus recruiters can view samples of writing, design projects, or entries documenting understanding of the importance of a global perspective, ethics, and so on—all in a multimedia format.

The RosE-Portfolio system is student driven, eliminating the need for faculty to be responsible for the collection of student material for submission. Faculty advisers have access to their advisees' portfolios for the purpose of reviewing their progress. Academic advisers receive periodic reports on the status of their advisees' portfolios. If a student has not submitted portfolio materials for a period of time, the adviser will receive an e-mail message asking her to encourage the student to submit materials prior to registering for classes the next quarter.

Faculty ratings of student portfolios provide assessment data that faculty can use to validate their own assessment efforts. In addition, the RosE-Portfolio allows development of department-specific folders that enable faculty to identify program-specific outcomes in addition to those that are general to all students.

Because the RosE-Portfolio can be accessed at any time from anywhere, we have the potential to involve our national board of advisers, alumni, and other constituent groups in the rating of portfolios. Inter-rater reliability could be established by bringing all raters together on campus for a half-day session, or rating could be done in small groups using video conferencing. Input from external constituents on the quality of student work would provide an assessment perspective that is not currently available.

Designing a Portfolio System for Your Campus

Portfolios, whether conventional or electronic, may not be the answer for every college or program. The decision to design an electronic portfolio system, however, will be driven by answers to the following questions:

What is the primary purpose of data collection? Portfolios can be used to assess an individual student's progress. They can be used to assess the growth of a student over time or take a showcase approach, in which students are told to submit material that represents their best work. Portfolios can also be sampled to determine whether program or institutional student outcome goals are being met.

What strategies are you going to use to assess the material submitted in the portfolios? A clear plan must be developed for categorizing and assessing the material in a meaningful, focused way that is relevant to the purpose of portfolio use. Scoring rubrics must be constructed and ease of access for rating purposes must be considered in the design.

If you plan to use portfolios for program assessment, answers to the following questions will guide development of the process.

Will you assess everything in every student's portfolio? For a large program, as well as for purposes of program evaluation, it may not be practical or necessary to assess every portfolio. Thus, consideration should be given to developing a mechanism to sample part of every portfolio.

Are you going to assess every goal and performance criterion every year or every semester? If you have 11 student outcomes to measure and each of these has an average of six performance criteria, there is a maximum of 66 submissions per student. If there are 100 students in the program, there are potentially 6,600 assessment data points. Common sense would dictate that you develop a plan to assess the portfolios that is based on sound sampling methodology. Sample the portfolios for potential problem areas (which of the performance outcomes appear to be the most problematic for students?), and develop an assessment schedule that maximizes the ability to identify areas for improvement early in the process. All outcomes should be assessed with the same rigor, but the results of that assessment will differ. When evidence indicates that students are having difficulty demonstrating a desired outcome at the appropriate level, improvements can be made in the processes designed to promote the outcome; then new assessments can be made. Outcomes requiring improvement can be assessed more frequently than the outcomes students consistently attain. The design of an electronic portfolio system can automate the search and sampling process.

What resources do you have available? Done properly, assessment takes time, money, and skill. The RosE-Portfolio is the culmination of two and a half years of planning, design, development, testing, improvement, and implementation involving many hours of faculty, staff, and student time. Portfolios may not be the most expedient method for assessing student outcomes, but there seems to be an inverse relationship between the quality of measurement methods and their expediency.

Summary

When assessing student outcomes, multiple methods should be considered. Portfolios can add breadth and depth of information that no other method provides. Developing an electronic portfolio system can reduce the number of disadvantages of portfolios and enhance the overall effectiveness of data collection, assessment, and subsequent improvement of academic programs.

References

Paulson, L. F., Paulson, P. R., and Meyer, C. "What Makes a Portfolio a Portfolio?" *Educational Leadership*, 1991, 48(5), 60–63.

Prus, J., and Johnson, R. "Assessment and Testing Myths and Realities." New Directions for Community Colleges, no. 88. San Francisco: Jossey-Bass, 1994.

Gloria M. Rogers is vice president for institutional resources and assessment and Timothy Chow is director of institutional research at Rose-Hulman Institute of Technology in Terre Haute, Indiana.

The Amsterdam Faculty of Education's Digital Portfolio

Jacqueline Kösters, Magda Ritzen

The electronic portfolio developed by the Amsterdam Faculty of Education is an excellent example of how portfolios can be used both as assessment and learning tools. This article describes what this e-portfolio looks like, how students learn to use it, and the ways it serves to promote student awareness of their own learning. From Assessment Update *12:5, September–October 2000.*

Since 1997 the Amsterdam Faculty of Education (EFA) has been recognized officially as a center for experimental teacher education. All of our students (about 6,000 total) have chosen upon entry to the university to become teachers in primary or secondary schools. In the four-year program, didactics and the subject they will be teaching are integrated. This article describes the development of our digital portfolio.

Educational Innovation at EFA

The key ingredient in the EFA vision of education is offering students an environment in which they must assume responsibility for the ways they acquire the necessary capacities for their profession (which are constantly changing) and for the ways they demonstrate these to the outside world. Within EFA, the skills needed for the profession are described as competences; competences define the way a teacher acts in a complex professional situation (for example, the field of education). A competence always implies the integration of knowledge and skills. Our competences are divided into three domains:

1. Teaching skills and methodology (linked to a particular subject area)

2. Working in a school organization

3. Functioning as a professional

Making the competences explicit allows students to be aware of what is required of them, to monitor their growth and development, and to justify the choices they make among the learning environments offered in the program.

Students work in learning practices—learning environments in which students are responsible for providing a product or service, which where possible is based on a commission from the professional field. EFA faculty plan eventually to offer a broad range of learning practices from which students can choose, depending on the learning goals they want to achieve. This means that we must make clear from the outset the main competences to be gained in the learning practices.

The program element known as metawork has the function of guiding students in the learning process; it provides cohesion in the curriculum. During metawork, students become aware of and develop their metacognitive skills; their experiences and work in the learning practices are instrumental in this development. A mentor, who supervises the metawork, guides students in the choices they make and in the process of formulating learning goals and linking them to the required competences. The mentor also guides students in preparing evidence to show mastery of the competences in the integrative assessments. During metawork, students practice the presentation of their portfolios in order to show their progress.

From the start of their studies, students are divided into metawork groups. Each group meets once a week for the first two years under the mentor's supervision. In the later years, students are expected to have acquired sufficient metacognitive skills to render the intensive weekly sessions with the mentor unnecessary.

During the program, an integrative assessment takes place on three occasions:

- At the end of the foundation year (to ascertain if the student is ready for the second year of the program)
- Before the long placement in the fourth year (similarly, to judge student readiness)
- At the end of the program (to award qualified teacher status)

Assessments are based on the definitions of the competences. For each competence, at each of the three assessments, criteria are formulated that students must attain to be considered ready to start the next level of the program, the long placement, or their professional career. During the assessment, students must demonstrate to a committee of assessors that they have reached the necessary level and they must make their learning process visible. At the end of the foundation year, the committee consists of EFA faculty; the other assessments also involve assessors from outside EFA. The roles of mentor and assessor are strictly separated; mentors never assess their own students. To provide evidence, students use their portfolios; they make selections from the products and reflection reports they have collected there. The assessors then study the evidence provided by the student in the portfolio and formulate feedback. The student has an opportunity to respond to this feedback, with the help of the portfolio.

The student also has to carry out a number of complex practical assignments on the spot.

The Portfolio

The EFA portfolio is a multifunctional instrument used in metawork and assessment. It functions in the following ways:

- Promotes awareness of competences
- Aids in reflection
- Helps in designing and documenting a student's individual program
- Assists students in making choices and setting goals and thus in managing their learning themselves
- Serves as an assessment tool

EFA has chosen to have a digital portfolio in the form of an individual home page for each student. A digital portfolio makes it possible to arrange a great deal of material clearly and compactly. Through hyperlinks, students can easily show the relationships between different parts of the portfolio and thus demonstrate coherence among different elements in the program.

In developing the portfolio concept, we felt the need to offer students the freedom to develop their own portfolio, but we also felt it necessary to offer them a fixed structure. The portfolio is, most important, an instrument belonging to the student; students use it to direct their learning process and to reflect on their development and growth. The portfolio must never be allowed to become a mere form to be filled in. At the same time, the faculty must keep an eye on students' development and progress. A portfolio must provide the instructor and assessors with evidence that a student has insight into his or her learning process and possesses the competences. Therefore we have decided to make a number of elements in the portfolio compulsory for all students. Within this compulsory framework students are free to assemble their portfolios however they wish.

In the portfolio, these menu items are always visible on the screen: Opening Page, Curriculum Vitae, Products, Competences, Presentations, Overviews, Links, E-mail Address, Tools.

On the Opening Page of the portfolio, a student can introduce himself with a photo or short text.

The Curriculum Vitae gives an overview of the student's education and work experience, as well as all the learning practices that have been followed. Students are also encouraged to include extracurricular activities that contribute to development of the competences.

In the Products section, students include all the products they have created during their EFA career and possibly elsewhere: It is an archive of products. At least as important as the product itself are the contract and justification the student writes to accompany each product. In the contract, the student records in advance which individual learning objectives she will work at in a learning practice and how she would like to be assessed on these objectives. In the justification, the student describes and analyzes her learning process, including feedback from instructors and fellow students, and formulates new learning goals.

The Competences section includes all competences related to the teaching profession. Students must prove that they possess these. They do this by reflecting regularly (at least once every 10 weeks) on their progress in the various competences through referring to products, and justifications accompanying products, by means of hyperlinks. The competences thus play a role in the student's self-assessment.

In Presentations, students select products and reflections to represent each competence. In other words, they use hyperlinks to create a path through the portfolio. In this way, the student can make presentations for different purposes—for example, an application for a long placement or an integrative assessment. The starting point for a presentation is a self-evaluation, or strengths and weaknesses analysis, with regard to progress on each competence.

Overviews are examples of learning practices and their assessments. Students can't rewrite this part.

The Links section contains links to other Web sites. It includes descriptions of learning practices, approved contracts stating student learning goals, and assessments and any other information relevant for EFA students and staff. Students can also add links to Web sites that they think are important for fellow students.

E-mail Address gives the student's electronic contact information.

Tools contains some portfolio tools, including, among others, selection of language (Dutch or English), format for a contract, competence meters, and an authorization tool (students can screen off parts of the portfolio and allow access only for people who are known in the network environment).

A portfolio information site has been developed to support students and instructors. Here they can find all the information needed about portfolios and their use. The contents of this site include a portfolio user's guide, a guide to designing Web pages, sample portfolios, and hyperlinks to relevant Web sites.

In the foundation year, students' portfolios are available only via the EFA intranet; in subsequent years, students may decide to put their portfolios on the World Wide Web.

Instructors and mentors are encouraged to create their own portfolios so that they can experience the same process as their students.

Implementation of the Portfolio

The pilot year of the project included two of the five functions of the portfolio described earlier—promoting awareness of the competences and aiding reflection. Experience with the pilot project made it clear that reflecting on the competences is useful only if they are recognizable in the curriculum and the portfolio provides latitude for students' own ideas about form and content.

During the pilot year, mentors, students, and others involved in the project met regularly to discuss the function and contents of the portfolios. In these meetings, the functions and layout of portfolios developed elsewhere also were examined. The experience gained with the pilot project and the ideas expressed in the various meetings were formulated as requirements for the portfolio. On the basis of these global requirements, students from different subject areas made three trial portfolios. A single prototype was then developed. This prototype was shown to all those involved and formed the starting point for a detailed description of what a portfolio should look like, what it should be able to do, and how it should be realized technically.

In the second year of the project, three departments worked with a pilot integrative assessment in which students used portfolios to show that they met the competence criteria for the first year.

Students now receive training during the first teaching period (10 weeks) that encompasses all the skills necessary for designing and creating their own portfolio. Later in the year, a course that presents more advanced Web editors is provided for those who find the possibilities provided by Frontpage Express too limited.

More information on working with portfolios can be found on our Web site. This information is freely available to all, in Dutch as well as in English. The EFA portfolio site is at <http://portfolioinfo.efa.nl>. The EFA Web site at <http://www.efa.nl> includes some English articles about EFA's dynamic curriculum.

Jacqueline Kösters is a professor at the Amsterdam Faculty of Education. Magda Ritzen is senior consultant at the Faculty of Economy, Utrecht.

Student Portfolios: Effective Academic Advising Tools

Arthur C. Hessler, Susan Kuntz

Here is another, less obvious, use of portfolios. This article describes a pilot program for using portfolios in academic advising to help students make decisions about what to study, understand where they need to improve their learning, and better explore their own interests and abilities. From Assessment Update 4:6, November-December 1992.

Much of the recent emphasis on assessment is on outcomes: what students know at the end of a course of study. But this means of assessment does not tell students how to improve. We need to know what is behind outcomes. The portfolio means of assessment builds on rather than dismisses the daily assignments, course papers, and exams that are the ongoing work of students and teachers. The portfolio documents academic growth. It indicates not only where students end up but how they got there.

The portfolio method of assessment offers policy makers, teachers, and students a way of examining the outcome of student work as it relates to the curriculum, academic advising, and student input in the learning process. It views learning as a process that takes place over time with the assistance of several elements.

Portfolios can be used for many purposes. The collection of materials invites conversation about its contents. With the portfolio as a tool, we can give students in-depth feedback and advising. Informed decisions can be made as to courses of study to pursue, skill areas that need improvement, and the match between interests and abilities. The portfolio also encourages more in-depth conversations about curriculum and the match between institutional mission and goals.

Collegewide assessment was initiated at Saint Michael's College in the fall of 1990, beginning with entering first-year students. In August, sixty of these incoming students, thirty who had declared majors and thirty who were undeclared, were asked to volunteer for a pilot project on portfolio assessment in academic advising. Our intent in the pilot portfolio project was twofold: to learn whether the portfolio enhanced students' perceptions of the quality of the academic advice they received and advisers' perceptions of the quality of academic advice they were able to provide.

We attempted to use portfolios as indicators of performance over time that would inform academic advisers of student academic progress or lack thereof. The sixty student volunteers were subdivided among twelve academic advisers, half by specific discipline and the other half to faculty trained to advise undeclared students. Many of the twelve advisers had other advisees, but for the purposes of this study, they were instructed not to initiate portfolio advising with those students. Portfolio advisers were directed to meet their advisees at preregistration time and on at least two other occasions during each semester. At each of these meetings, student performance and portfolio contents, as an indicator of that performance, were discussed.

Portfolio contents included a values-goals questionnaire; scored writing sample and content assessment tests that were completed by all first-year students at the beginning of the fall semester; and examples of papers— including drafts, laboratory reports, examinations, and score sheets—as they were accumulated from courses. At the end of the year, a written self-assessment of academic and co-curricular experiences was added.

In April, a questionnaire titled Student Perceptions of Academic Advising was distributed to fifty-five remaining portfolio students, to fifty-five first-year students who were not part of the project, and to sixty sophomores, sixty juniors, and sixty seniors, the latter all randomly selected. Students were asked to respond to the statement "Overall my academic adviser does an excellent job"; rating options ranged from 5 ("strongly agree") to 1 ("strongly disagree"). Mean values were as follows: portfolio first-year students, 4.65 (twenty-nine respondents); nonportfolio first-year students, 3.57 (twenty-six respondents); sophomores, 4.09 (twenty-two respondents); juniors, 3.97 (thirty-seven respondents); and seniors, 4.14 (thirty-five respondents).

Clearly, first-year students who were advised with portfolio assistance perceived the quality of advising to be better than did nonportfolio students in general, including upper-class students who presumably would have formed closer relationships with their academic advisers. This perceived difference was significant at the 0.005 level.

Other items that exhibited significance at the 0.01 level or less included office hour availability, academic schedule planning, concern about academic progress, discussion of academic interests, discussion of career and individual goals, and several other issues pertaining to the adviser's knowledge about college policies. The results on knowledge about college policies we attribute to the greater amount of time spent by the portfolio advisees discussing academics with the adviser, not to a difference in advisers. The faculty academic advisers of Saint Michael's are generally considered excellent, and thus there is qualitative support for attributing the differences between portfolio and nonportfolio students to the portfolios as opposed to variability among academic advisers.

Ten of the twelve portfolio faculty advisers had both portfolio and nonportfolio advisees and thus were able to make direct comparisons between the two groups of students. Faculty perceptions suggest that use of portfolios enhances their general knowledge of students and the quality of their academic advice.

In response to a statement about their "opportunity to provide academic advice," the advisers' mean for portfolio advised students was 4.0, for nonportfolio-advised students, 3.0. In response to the statement "In getting to know the student, does the portfolio promote dialogue?" The advisers' mean for portfolio students was 4.2 and for nonportfolio students, 2.8. Faculty comments about time commitment included "It takes more time to initiate meetings"; "More time is required to review portfolios"; "It takes more time, but it's quality time"; "It's been a big plus; I know my portfolio advisees much better and students come in more often just to talk."

Grade-point averages from the portfolio and nonportfolio first-year students were compared at the end of both the fall and spring semesters. Given the positive perceptions of advisees and advisers alike of the portfolio advising process, it did not seem unreasonable to expect portfolio students to have higher grade-point averages than nonportfolio students, especially for the spring semester when the benefits of fall portfolio advising might have been expected to pay dividends. In actuality, there were no significant differences, either in aggregate grade-point average or letter-grade distribution. Fall semester and spring semester grade point averages for portfolio-advised first year students were 2.531 and 2.571, respectively; for nonportfolio-advised students, 2.502 and 2.500, respectively. We interpret this result as an indication of the generally high quality of academic advice provided by all academic advisers, be they assisted by portfolios or not. Portfolio advisee and adviser perceptions of the quality of academic advice were very positive, but in the pilot project, portfolios did not appear to contribute to significantly better grades for the students who used them.

The pilot project at Saint Michael's suggests that portfolios can enhance the effectiveness of academic advising. In our experience thus far, a portfolio:

- Increases students' perceptions that they are receiving quality academic advice
- Directs students to be reflective about changes in their academic performance over time
- Provides faculty advisers with evidence of student performance to inform academic advising
- Enhances adviser-advisee dialogue
- Is more time-intensive for both adviser and student
- Is relatively easy and cost-effective to implement.

We plan to pilot-test portfolios for another year with an additional sixty first-year students. The first pilot year provided an excellent learning experience for us as coordinators. An important area in which we need to improve our efforts is in orienting both the faculty advisers and the student volunteers. Some students who had agreed to participate did so only minimally, meeting with the faculty adviser only twice—at pre-registration times—during the year. The invitation to participate must define expectations much more clearly than the letter that was sent during the first year.

Similarly, faculty advisers must be more assertive with their portfolio advisees about the importance of meetings. Advisers also need a better understanding of portfolio organization and content and subsequent use of academic advising. A workshop is planned for the faculty advisers, and they and the portfolio students will meet as a group with the assessment coordinator early in the fall for an overview of the portfolio process.

As we continue to learn, portfolio assessment will become an integral aspect of ongoing institutional assessment at Saint Michael's.

Arthur C. Hessler is associate academic dean and Susan Kuntz is director of graduate programs in education at Saint Michael's College in Colchester, Vermont.

Electronic Portfolios
for Accreditation?

Trudy W. Banta

Indiana Unversity-Purdue University Indianapolis is one of six urban institutions experimenting with the use of electronic portfolios to demonstrate student learning and institutional effectiveness. This article describes how this experiment is going, the benefits of using portfolios, and some of the unanswered questions. From Assessment Update 15:4, July-August 2003.

In recent years there has been a growing interest in using electronic portfolios to demonstrate accountability and student learning. Many, many important details still need to be worked out—appropriate content, privacy issues, and costs, among them. But early adopters are paving the way, and everything we know about the rapidly increasing sophistication of technology suggests that the electronic portfolio finally may offer us the authentic evidence of current status as well as growth and development over time that those of us involved in outcomes assessment have sought for decades.

Since 1998, when funding for six urban institutions to pursue the Urban Universities Portfolio Project (UUPP) was provided by the Pew Charitable Trusts, my institution, Indiana University-Purdue University Indianapolis (IUPUI) has been experimenting with electronic portfolios for demonstrating student learning and institutional effectiveness. When the UUPP ended in 2001, California State University, Sacramento; Georgia State University; IUPUI; Portland State University; University of Illinois at Chicago; and the University of Massachusetts Boston had developed prototypes for institutional portfolios that would make the work of each of these institutions more accessible to their stakeholders and to the public.

Of the six UUPP institutions, IUPUI was closest in time to its next regional reaccreditation review. So in 2001 Susan Kahn, the national

UUPP director, and Sharon Hamilton, the campus UUPP coordinator, began work with Karen Black, Victor Borden, and others on whom I rely for assistance with planning and assessment on adapting the IUPUI portfolio to a web-based self study for reaccreditation by the North Central Association (NCA). By the time our NCA visiting team arrived on November 18, 2002, we had completed the self study, which readers of *Assessment Update* may view at www.iport.iupui.edu. NCA staff informed us that as of that date IUPUI had submitted the most extensively Web-based self study they had received.

The electronic portfolio enabled us to illustrate points in our narrative self study by linking to a wide variety of evidence. We chose to focus a special emphasis self study on each of two essential elements of IUPUI's mission: teaching and learning and civic engagement. In connection with the narrative on teaching and learning we illustrated the changing demographic characteristics of our students by linking to tables and graphs displaying ten-year trends. In making other points we used trend data from student and alumni surveys and our students' responses on the National Survey of Student Engagement as compared with those of students at other urban universities. We linked to matrices designed to show how faculty in each college are teaching and assessing learning in connection with each of our six Principles of Undergraduate Learning. And there are other materials that provide evidence of the uses faculty in each of the colleges have made over the last decade based on assessment findings. Moving to the level of the individual student, we illustrated the assessment of student writing by showing a graded theme with the rubric used for grading and faculty comments that pop up with a click of the mouse. Finally, there is a short videotape of a student making a speech at the beginning of her first speech course and another clip showing her last speech; the scoring rubric and how it was used to grade these performances accompanies this illustration.

For the self study on civic engagement we indicated at the outset that we were at a very early stage in assessing our effectiveness. Nevertheless, we demonstrated a new tool, the Civic Engagement Inventory, that we have designed to enable faculty and staff to report on various community projects, including evaluative data that show the impact of the work. We invited our consultant-evaluators on the North Central visiting team to help us think through a number of issues we need to address with respect to civic engagement and the assessment thereof.

We provided access via the Web to almost every document identified in the NCA criteria for accreditation. When members of the visiting team arrived on campus they found in addition to a laptop for each, only about six inches of shelf space devoted to printed materials—some financial audit reports not made available electronically. This compares to the bookcases full of documents an institution of our size usually makes available to reviewers.

In the decade since IUPUI's last NCA review in 1992 we have developed an office of planning, evaluation, and improvement that has linked performance indicators to campus goals and drawn much of the information for these indicators from academic and administrative units' annual reports, which are based on unit goals that are aligned with campus goals. Had we not elected to develop two special emphasis self studies, the IUPUI report for reaccreditation could have been drawn with little additional effort from unit and campus annual reports. With these resources already in place, the out-of-pocket expenses associated with the 2002 self study were only a third of those recorded in 1992. Moreover, just as we were able to involve hundreds, if not thousands, of faculty, staff, students, and community stakeholders in reviewing and commenting on our developing selfstudy without the expense of duplicating a copy for each, now we can share that work with you without incurring the cost of mailing it to you.

Obviously we thought we were building a better mousetrap with the institutional electronic portfolio as our self study for reaccreditation. We believed we could provide more authentic evidence of our accomplishments, with more depth and breadth, using the multiple types of media available through the Web. We were pleased that we could involve many more stakeholders as critics during the self study process than would have been possible using a paper format. We found that faculty and administrators were able to see more connections between their own work and that in other units as our story developed on the Web. Thus we believe we contributed some openings in those silo walls that traditionally separate individual units. We certainly discovered some missing structures and linkages that we now know we need to build. And through the process we expanded the pool of faculty and administrators who have a broad vision of the campus and its potential.

Following their visit, the NCA review team confirmed some of our beliefs about the value of the electronic institutional portfolio. They noted:

- the dynamic, rich quality of the information provided
- the direct links to evidence and illustrations of key points that enhanced the persuasiveness of points made in the narrative
- the efficient connections that were apparent between related or overlapping elements
- the transparence of the evidence, which made the team's job of vouching for the institution's integrity much easier

But the team also noted some negative aspects of the web-based self study. We had predicted that by having all the usual reference material available via Web links, we would save the team time on campus; we thought the reviewers would spend less time reading and gathering basic information and more time interacting with people who could give them first-hand accounts. Their questionnaire responses indicated that the team members did not agree that we had saved them time for personal interactions while they were with us.

We were surprised to learn that the search feature we incorporated was not often used. The same was true for the annual assessment reports from the academic units!

As is inevitably the case, some of our Web links did not work. In addition to identifying that as a source of frustration, the reviewers asked for "boundaries" on linked material; in some cases we sent them to a link, they got lost there, and once they found their way back to the self study, they wondered why they had been led astray! They told us to do more summarizing, highlighting, and prioritizing.

This last recommendation—a source of deep frustration for pioneers that we hope will be addressed for those who follow us on this path—stemmed in part from the fact that we were asked to provide a narrative self study on paper in addition to that on the Web. Since the paper copy needed to be able to stand on its own, we had to put most of the narrative on the Web and simply add links to it there. If we had been at liberty to use the Web version alone, we indeed could have done more "summarizing, highlighting, and prioritizing."

I have saved the most telling comment for last. Even though members chosen for IUPUI's review team were told at the outset that the self study would be Web-based and were asked specifically if they could work within that context, almost half of the respondents relied primarily on the printed copy of the self-study!

Is the electronic institutional portfolio really the way accreditation self studies will be done in the future? Does having more material available on the Web increase the time required for review prior to the visit beyond that which most reviewers can commit? Must we continue to prepare a traditional narrative with links so that in the end we can print it and send a paper copy to the review team? Admittedly, the paper copy makes it easier to highlight passages, make marginal notes, and mark a page worthy of a quick return. Or might we be allowed to take full advantage of the capacity of the Web to use a picture to convey a thousand words? Clearly, our experience has left us with a number of nagging questions.

How Can Portfolios Be Scored?

How Portfolios Show Us Problems with Holistic Scoring, but Suggest an Alternative

Peter Elbow

The author argues that a collection of writing samples in a portfolio gives a much more accurate picture of a student's writing abilities than does a single essay that has been scored by conventional holistic methods. From Assessment Update 6:4, July-August 1994.

Portfolios significantly improve our assessment of student writing because they significantly improve validity. That is, portfolios give us so much more trustworthy a picture of that ability. But when portfolios enhance validity, they also undermine reliability. Let me explain.

When most people ask, "How good a writer is this student?" they are really asking two distinct questions. On the one hand, they are asking, "What are the student's strengths and weaknesses?" Portfolios give us a much more accurate and trustworthy picture of strengths and weaknesses than we can get by looking at single papers from a classroom or an examination. Portfolios give us a good indication of which genres of writing someone is better and worse at (for example, narration versus persuasion versus explanation of complex data versus memo versus lyric poem), and which skills or abilities someone is better and worse at (for example, boundless invention versus clear organization versus good revising versus clear syntax versus lively and characteristic voice). On the other hand, most people are, unfortunately, also asking, "What number can I give this student?" They want a single grade or holistic score so that all students can be ranked along a single dimension. (Or at least this is true in most academic and legislative settings. Actual writers and literary critics tend, in fact, to mean something much more complex than a number when they talk about how good a writer someone is. This in itself ought to make us wary of single numbers.)

Portfolios do not give us a better picture of how good a writer is if what we have in mind is a number. In a sense, they give a more diverse picture than we get from single essays. If we look only at single pieces of writing, all answering the same question and written under the same conditions, all in the same genre to the same audience, we are much more likely to agree with one another in our holistic numerical rankings. When a portfolio gives us a collection of diverse pieces by each writer, and one writer's selection of pieces is different from that of another writer, it is inappropriate to think we can trust a single holistic score with which we pretend to sum up this diversity of performances by each writer and compare all writers along a single quantitative scale. If the story and the personal writing were strong and expository, and the argumentative and analytical pieces were weak, what score does this add up to? Readers will differ according to their values.

Until the publication of the research by Despain and Hilgers (1992), I was more worried that the success of portfolios might lull people into further complacency about interreader reliability. In fact, portfolios may now finally give us the leverage we have needed to dislodge our overreliance on holistic scoring in general: our habit of using single numbers to rank complex performances along a single dimension. The diversity of pieces in a portfolio simply makes more obvious what is just as true of single pieces: Diversity of features or qualities exists in any complex performance, and readers who are not scoring in conformity to a scoring guide simply do not agree on a single score, even for single pieces. A number of us have been arguing that the high-reliability results in the scoring of single pieces of writing are really epiphenomenal. They are a product of the training that gets readers to agree in ways they would never agree in normal reading.

It would be excessively pure and politically useless to argue that we should avoid all holistic scoring, all bottom-line, single-number evaluation. We are wiser, on both theoretical and practical grounds, if we can find ways to make our thinking complex and answerable to pragmatic institutional and cultural needs. Portfolio assessment may be able to come to the rescue here and have a paradoxical influence on our thinking about quantification. Portfolios show us the absurdity of holistic scoring as it is currently practiced, with scales from 1 to 6, but at the same time they also suggest the virtue of a peculiarly crude, simple, minimal kind of holistic scoring.

The way in which portfolios undermine conventional holistic scoring is through their capaciousness as containers: They present us with "mixed bags" that we do not have to face with single pieces of writing, bags that are too mixed for a single number. Human performance varies from occasion to occasion, and single pieces of writing shield us from that variability. But what if the portfolio bag is not so mixed? What about a full and rich portfolio where most readers agree that most of the pieces are excellent? Are we not then more than usually justified in calling the writer very strong? Similarly, what if most readers agree that most of the pieces are very poor or unsatisfactory? Are we not more than usually justified in calling the writer weak?

My suggestion then, is that portfolio assessment might justify giving two holistic scores: "excellent" and "poor/unsatisfactory." It might be called a theoretical scandal to give holistic scores to a few portfolios at the margins and no scores to the rest, yet it could also be described as theoretical wisdom to give holistic scores only to those portfolios where a single-number verdict has any justification, and to refuse to give indefensible scores to that whole range of portfolios about which readers cannot agree. The data from Despain and Hilgers (1992) show that readers had the most disagreement about middle-range papers, and also that their middle scores were often averages of higher and lower ones on different papers. Middle rankings depend on a concatenation of accidents: the weighing of different genres and features as specified by the test leaders, or random compromises among readers' conflicting standards and weightings.

Such a practice of minimal or marginal holistic scoring can be bolstered on pragmatic grounds. That is, sometimes we really do need a single bottom-line verdict, namely, a holistic score. In certain circumstances, we need to decide which students should be denied a place if we have limited resources or denied credit, or required to repeat a course or to take a preparatory course. Sometimes we also need to decide which students should get an award or scholarship. And if enough readers agree that certain work is good, that work will probably serve as a helpful example to others. These decisions about excellence or weakness can never be wholly fair, but they are much fairer, much more secure and justified, than most of the holistic scores we now give, especially all those fine-grained rankings in the middle range.

Speaking of pragmatism, this minimal holistic scoring cuts testing time and costs at least in half. It is the procedure used at Stony Brook, and we discovered that most portfolios can be read very quickly. Readers are looking only for strikingly good or bad portfolios. Most portfolios soon disqualify themselves—by having too much weakness to be excellent or too much strength to be terrible. What a pleasure to save all the money we normally spend on giving indefensible and misleading scores. (For more information about this topic, see Elbow, 1994.)

References

Despain, L., and Hilgers, T. L. "Readers' Responses to the Rating of Non-Uniform Portfolios: Are There Limits of Portfolios' Utility?" WPA: Writing Program Administration, 1992, 16 (1–2), 24–37.

Elbow, P. "Will the Virtues of Portfolios Blind Us to Their Potential Dangers?" In D. Daiker, L. Black, M. Morenberg, and J. Sommers (eds.), New Directions in Portfolio Assessment. Portsmouth, N.H.: Heinemann/Boynton-Cook, 1994.

Peter Elbow is professor of English at the University of Massachusetts, Amherst.

Portfolio Sorting—A Description and Application

Charles W. Spurr, Michael J. Kiphart, Betty Jo Miller

How can portfolios be scored effectively? This article provides detailed information on a method known as sorting—a method that looks like a variation on holistic scoring, but without the pitfalls described by Peter Elbow in the previous article. From Assessment Update 9:2, *March-April, 1997.*

Portfolio sorting is a method for assessing change over time. This assessment tool, developed and first used at Saint Mary's College of Maryland in 1995, can be used to investigate a wide array of assessment factors, can be used with outside raters, provides quantifiable results, and is relatively easy to implement. In this article, we provide a description of portfolio sorting and an example of its use.

General Description

Portfolio sorting involves the sorting of pairs of portfolio items into "better" and "worse" stacks according to the quality of some specified factor. For example, a rater might be asked to review a pair of essays for the quality of grammar. After reviewing the pair, the rater would place the essay having the better grammar into the better stack and the essay having the poorer grammar into the worse stack. Following this initial sort, the rater would be handed another pair of essays and asked, once again, to determine which essay contains the better grammar. While sorting, the rater is not aware that each essay within a pair was written by the same student— one essay as a first-year student and the other essay as a senior.

An analysis of the resulting better and worse stacks provides a basis for assessment. If no difference exists between first-year and senior essays in terms of grammar, there will be, on average, as many first-year essays in the better stack as there are senior essays. If grammar skills improve between the first and senior years, the better grammar stack should be composed mainly of senior essays. Hence, the null hypothesis of central concern is that first-year and senior essays are equally represented within the better stack. The corresponding alternative hypothesis is that there is a difference in the representation of first-year and senior essays within the better stack. Statistical tests are performed to determine if the composition of the better and the worse stacks differs significantly from a 50–50 mixture of first-year and senior essays.

While this example used grammar, portfolio sorting permits considerable flexibility in the range of characteristics being assessed. For example, written essays might also be sorted on the basis of such factors as organization and critical thinking. Recorded performances might be sorted on phrasing, instrumental technique, and so on. Paintings might be sorted on technique or composition.

Portfolio Item Pairs. Great care must be taken to ensure that portfolio items are appropriate for comparison. In general, first-year and senior items should be similar to each other in terms of format, medium, language, topic, type of assignment, and so on. For example, if samples of writing are compared for organization, it would be inappropriate to compare a lab report with a short story, or a poem with a written narrative. Ensuring item similarity beforehand helps the rater concentrate on evaluating the assessment factor and also helps ensure that the composition of item pairs is not biased toward any particular outcome.

Raters. To enhance the credibility of this assessment tool, raters should not be affiliated with the institution or those who do not possess knowledge of the portfolio or assessment process. Nevertheless, raters should have the expertise, academic or professional, to render credible judgments concerning the assessment factors. Finally, several raters should be employed to make sure that judgments can be obtained reliably.

Optional Refinement. Raters may also be asked to assign a quality grade to each of the portfolio items being sorted. Thus, in addition to determining *if* a change has occurred, portfolio sorting may be used to determine *how much* of a change has occurred.

Portfolio Sorting: An Application

Assessment at Saint Mary's College of Maryland is overseen by an assessment committee and involves several assessment techniques. Student portfolios, which contain representative works from each general education course as obtained from a stratified random sample of students, form a major component of the assessment program at Saint Mary's. This portfolio collection program has been in effect for five years, thereby enabling us to compare pairs of first-year and senior portfolio items.

Most of the portfolio items at Saint Mary's are written essays. Given the limited number of first-year and senior papers available for sorting, the assessment committee decided to limit its investigation to the following five factors: clarity of thinking, critical thinking, grammar and usage, organization, and substance. Written definitions for each of these factors were developed for use by the raters.

Portfolio Item Pairs. Several steps were taken to make sure that item pairs were fairly constructed for portfolio sorting. First, portfolios were examined for first-year and senior items that were reasonable to compare. Second, a random numbers generator was used to assign each available item pair to one of the five assessment categories for sorting. Third, the fairness and unbiased nature of the random assignments were verified. Finally, two additional college employees performed independent reviews of the resulting item pairs and category assignments to verify that the item pairs were fairly constructed for sorting. Using this procedure, five first year–senior item pairs were assigned to each of the five assessment categories for sorting; hence, twenty-five first year–senior item pairs were used in this portfolio sorting session.

To protect the identity of portfolio students, names and dates were removed from all item pairs and replaced by coded identification labels. Each label indicated the assessment category (*clarity of thinking* through *substance*), the item pair within the category (1 through 5), and whether a paper was obtained during the first year or senior year (triangles and circles were randomly assigned as class codes, with approximately half of the first-year papers receiving a triangle code and approximately half receiving a circle code). An example of an identification label for the first-year paper of the third item pair to be compared for *grammar* is "grammar, 3, Δ", where the triangle is the randomly assigned symbol indicating the first year.

Raters. Five raters were employed in the present study. Three of the raters were not affiliated with the college (a newspaper columnist, a minister, and an archaeologist), and two of the raters were college administrators who were not involved with teaching or aware of the portfolio-assessment process (we fell short of the ideal of having all outside raters). All five had a baccalaureate degree, four had a master's degree, and one had a doctorate. The three outside raters were paid $100 each for their participation.

Sorting Session. Portfolio sorting occurred on campus in a single session involving all five raters. The moderator opened the session by reading a set of instructions to the raters, who were seated around a conference table. These instructions were extremely vague about the purpose of the meeting but promised a full explanation at the end of the session. Before the actual sorting began, a practice sorting trial was given to make sure that all raters understood the procedure.

Sorting occurred in five rounds, with each round devoted to one of the five assessment factors. A round began with the moderator distributing and reading aloud the definition of that round's assessment factor. Following any discussion of the definition, each rater was given a rating sheet and an item pair for sorting. Each rater then determined which essay was better in terms of the assessment factor and recorded his or her judgment by writing the identification code, a circle or triangle, in the appropriate space on the rating sheet. In addition, each rater was asked to record a letter quality grade (A, A–, B+, . . . F) on his or her rating sheet for each of the essays being sorted.

After sorting a pair of essays and recording his or her responses, each rater awaited a signal from the moderator before passing the item pair to the rater seated on the right. In this way, each item pair was passed around the table and received five evaluations—one by each rater. Once all item pairs had been sorted by each of the raters, rating sheets and item pairs were gathered and the next round, devoted to a different assessment factor, began.

At the completion of the five rounds, the raters were asked what they thought was the intended purpose of the session. None of the raters offered the correct interpretation, and, indeed, all seemed quite surprised when they were given an explanation.

Results

Statistical analyses revealed no significant differences between the portfolio and corresponding first-year-to-senior cohort groups in terms of race, sex, or cumulative grade point average. Analyses also revealed fairly high interrater reliability indices for sorting, with an overall percentage agreement score of 85% and an overall r_{tt} of .77.

According to the null hypothesis, the representation of first-year and senior papers should be approximately equal within the better and worse categories of sorted papers. Twenty-five quality decisions were made during each round of the present study; hence, on average and by chance alone, one-half, or 12.5 (that is, 0.5 x 25), of the better papers for each assessment factor should be first-year papers and one-half, or 12.5, should be senior papers. If, on the other hand, qualitative changes do occur between the first and senior years, then significantly more than half of the better papers will be senior (or, possibly, first-year) papers.

For statistical analysis, a "hit" was defined as the classification of a senior paper as better and its corresponding first-year paper as worse; conversely, a "miss" was defined as the classification of a senior paper as worse and its corresponding first-year paper as better. Chi-square tests performed on hit-and-miss rates revealed a significant quality improvement overall (across factors) as well as significant quality improvements for the individual factors of critical thinking and organization. No factor showed a significant decrease in quality between the first and senior years.

Paired t-tests were used to analyze the grades (converted to points) assigned to the first-year and senior papers. Average grades improved for every assessment factor, with significant improvements obtained overall and for the single factor critical thinking.

Discussion

Several points should be noted about portfolio sorting and the results obtained:

Time requirements: The amount of time required for each sorting round will vary by the type of assessment factor, the type of portfolio item, and the number of raters involved. For the present study involving five raters, rounds took, on average, one-half hour with some rounds occurring much faster (for example, grammar) than others (for example, critical thinking).

Raters: The raters in this study seemed quite interested and involved in the sorting task. They did not take breaks and reported that they enjoyed being on campus and helping with this project. A potential benefit of this methodology is that it can involve outside raters in an important college activity, thereby strengthening connections between the college and the surrounding community.

Before-and-after design. Ideally, the "before" portfolio item will be representative of the student's work before any training, and the "after" item representative of work at the completion of training. To the extent that portfolio items are gathered during intermediate phases (such as using a first-year essay obtained at the end of the year as the "before" item), the impact of the educational program may appear to be diminished. Usage of true before and after portfolio items is essential for obtaining an assessment of the full impact of a program of study.

The openness of the "sort according to factor X" task that forms the core of portfolio sorting permits the exploration of a virtually unlimited range of assessment factors. Through this technique, we might explore which factors are affected by a college education and which are not. We might delineate the impact of one curriculum (for example, liberal arts) versus another (for example, training for one of the professions). We might investigate the development of factors across years rather than on just a first-year–senior basis. We might compare the factor improvements obtained at different colleges or among different demographic groups, and then seek to understand the reasons for any obtained differences. Clearly, there are many issues to investigate, and portfolio sorting may provide a methodology for exploring the effects of a college education.

Charles W. Spurr is director of institutional research and assistant professor of psychology, Michael J. Kiphart is planning and academic affairs specialist with the Maryland Higher Education Commission, and Betty Jo Miller is assistant director of institutional research at Saint Mary's College of Maryland, Saint Mary's City.

Involving Community in Program Assessment

W. Tracy Dillon

As a number of the authors in this collection have observed, one of the challenges in implementing portfolio assessment is that reviewing portfolios can be time consuming. This article outlines an approach used by Portland State University—a contest—that enlists members of the business community in the work of reading and rating student portfolios in technical writing. This approach has the added benefit of obtaining valuable feedback from community stakeholders on the effectiveness of the technical writing curriculum. From Assessment Update 9:2, *March-April, 1997.*

Universities and colleges more than ever before are being asked to account for their outcomes in ways that legislators, industry, and the public can appreciate and understand. Policymakers and taxpayers want assurance that the higher education community's priorities match their own. Assessment offers an important opportunity for engaging these constituents in meaningful dialogue about higher education's contribution to social welfare. However, assessment proponents often acknowledge the importance of clarifying goals and expectations to the community but rarely rely on the community to help shape those goals and expectations. We all agree that community participation in the assessment process is vital but we rarely offer a strategy for bringing the community to the table. The assessment process described here represents one simple and effective approach toward solving this problem.

Portfolios Program Assessment

In 1990, Portland State University embraced its identity as an urban institution and revised its mission statement to emphasize connections between the university and various constituents in the surrounding metropolitan community. Because the region is a popular and growing area for technical industries such as semiconductor manufacturers and chemical and environmental engineering groups, the university's professional writing program was positioned to contribute to the urban mission. Liaisons with local firms could enhance the education of writing students by creating internships and other community-based learning opportunities while providing local business with needed technical and business writing support.

As administrator of the professional writing program, I formed a corporate advisory board so that the employers who hire technical writers could help shape program goals. In the case of communication disciplines like technical and business writing, advisory boards facilitate internship and career enhancing contacts for students and increase program credibility and visibility in addition to improving curriculum planning (Ganahl and Ganahl, 1992; Winsor, 1992; Barclay, 1991). For technical writing programs especially, advisory board participation effectively bridges the gap between classroom and workplace (Barclay, 1991) and benefits board members as well as students and faculty (Brockman, 1982). Serving on such a board represents an effective networking opportunity for professionals who otherwise might not be able to contribute to local educational objectives.

My strategy involved modifying an accepted classroom assessment technique—the annotated portfolio (see Angelo and Cross, 1993)—for use in a contest. I wrote to presidents and chief executive officers of targeted companies asking them to help me determine what communication skills are necessary for success in the local business community by identifying key people in their organizations who were interested in assessing student writing. Representatives from Arthur Andersen, Cascade Earth Sciences, CH2M Hill, First Interstate Bank, The Harris Group, Intel, Sequent, and Tektronix participated in the first contest, awarding cash prizes donated from the companies. More important, each representative committed to an ongoing relationship.

The board's primary purpose is to offer advice regarding curriculum development, including course content and offerings. The annual assessment of student portfolios anchors this process. Each spring the board meets collectively to determine first-, second-, and third-place portfolio winners following a holistic writing assessment procedure. The portfolios provide a touchstone for important and ongoing dialogue about what works and what does not in technical and business writing. By evaluating and reacting to student writing, advisory board members identify standards and criteria for performance success, and I use this information to inform decision making about program goals and outcomes. The involvement of experts outside the university in determining these standards is a key feature of the assessment process and, at an urban university such as mine, at least, speaks to the larger institutional objective of building strong community partnerships.

As an adaptation of the annotated portfolio, the student portfolio proposed here gives the student writer primary control over the creative process. The portfolio represents a student's best work over time rather than simply giving a snapshot of a single performance and thus provides a more complete picture of writing competence. Most important, the portfolio provides a means for self-evaluation rather than simply giving contest judges a set of symptoms to evaluate. The student's annotations take the form of a cover letter that explains the rhetorical strategies and the communication context for each item in the portfolio. This letter also acts as an abstract that gives judges the background they need to evaluate the writing performance. Additionally, using the portfolio as a basis for a contest helps students realize that a well-prepared portfolio can contribute to the job search process. While most discussions of how to create and administer student portfolio assignments remain grounded in composition theory, the portfolio's potential benefit as an employment-gaining strategy receives almost exclusive attention in business communication pedagogy (see Aitken, 1994; Frick, 1994; Winter and Winter, 1992).

In my program, the portfolio contest is open to any enrolled student and is linked to the required Introduction to Technical Writing course, which integrates traditional portfolio assessment activities into the classroom learning experience. Students thus produce a portfolio early in their program and are encouraged to modify and develop it into an effective job application tool as they gain experience over time. The contest itself is open to students at any level, but generally those who enter are about to graduate, and their portfolios represent a wide array of technical and professional writing documents compiled from community-based as well as classroom activities. The portfolio thus is an important feature of the program, but students retain the choice of whether they wish to expand the assignment in the introductory course into a more formal document for later use, whether in the contest or in the job market.

Guidelines for Attracting and Maintaining an Advisory Board

Those interested in using a portfolio contest to attract and maintain an advisory board should remember three important guidelines. First, make participation important. The best way to do this involves placing the experience in the national context of reform in higher education. While potential advisory board members will appreciate an appeal for help in ensuring that students become contributing citizens in the local economy, emphasizing their contribution to a debate over the role and responsibility of higher education places the request in a larger social and political context. Linking portfolio assessment with the reform movement is particularly relevant since portfolios represent a somewhat new approach in contrast to standardized tests and multiple-choice exams. Part of the reform involves viewing each student learner as a unique human being, and portfolio work provides one of the best ways to capture the individuality of the student learner. Indeed, Courts and McInerney (1993), among others, argued that portfolio assessment is central to the reform movement.

Second, make participation easy. Simple and straightforward correspondence, including a stamped self-addressed return envelope, can encourage a potential board member to respond, for example. Provide response forms containing a checklist of alternative answers to the questions posed and fill-in blanks that a contact can complete quickly in lieu of writing a time-consuming letter of reply. When managing the portfolio contest, consider delivering portfolios on site at the judges' convenience and offering to make special arrangements if a potential judge becomes unavailable at contest time.

Finally, make participation lasting. This requires closing the assessment loop by giving feedback and follow-up to both judges and students. What these professionals say in evaluating student portfolios can inform decision making at many levels. Proper planning ensures a successful portfolio contest, and community contacts who choose to participate probably are dedicated to the spirit of assessment in the first place. If the contest succeeds, key people will have been identified who are willing to join an advisory board to help assess and shape program goals and outcomes. Maintaining their participation requires reminding them that their voice counts in the assessment process, and making it easy for them to be heard.

Monetary Considerations and Student Learning

Forming and maintaining an advisory board takes time, so one should consider whether one's institution will value the results as much as it would a published article or book. Here again, linking the work to the scholarship of assessment can justify the considerable expenditure of energy from a faculty development perspective. Also remember that no matter how many monetary contributions, internship opportunities, and other resources an advisory board creates, some colleagues will expect more. If board members donate a modest amount for the contest, why not get them to underwrite the entire program or to endow a department chair? Resist the pressure to make the relationship about money and remember that what makes it important is assessment. The end result of participation with an advisory board must be a payoff in student learning. Administrators may want dollars, but the process proposed here aims at soliciting ideas. A slow and steady building of relationships with advisory board members over time will do more to prepare students for success after graduation than will any one-time cash cow.

This final problem moves from logistical to philosophical concerns. While one contingent of colleagues may view ties with corporate partners as a means of harvesting dollars, an equally strong opposition may regard the entire enterprise as a sellout and may interpret any attempt to give the business community a voice in planning curriculum as an attempt to substitute training for education. But this assumption perpetuates the very stereotyping that has led constituents outside the university to think of assessment solely as a means of demanding accountability. From the constituents' perspective, academics are self-involved theorists who are more concerned with personal research agendas than with social welfare. From the academics' perspective, corporate types are money-mongering pragmatists who are more concerned with bottom lines than with expanding minds. Such attitudes preclude common goals and must be overcome if we are to use assessment to change and improve the perception of higher education in this country.

An effective assessment process ought to stimulate dialogue between the university and other parts of the community who seek to share the burden of preparing people for success and life-long learning. Individuals who are dedicated to this ideal exist in many institutions, not just universities, and they can and do contribute to student learning. The process described here offers one example of how to find such partners.

References

Aitken, J. E. "Assessment in Specific Programs: Employment, Program, and Course Student Portfolios in Communication Studies." Paper presented at the Speech Communication Summer Conference, Alexandria, Virginia, Aug. 1994.

Angelo, T. A., and Cross, K. P. *Classroom Assessment Techniques: A Handbook for College Teachers.* (2nd ed.) San Francisco: Jossey-Bass, 1993.

Barclay, R. O. "Technical Communication in the International Workplace: Some Implications for Curriculum Development." *Technical Communication,* 1991, *38* (3), 324–335.

Brockman, R. J. "Advisory Boards in Technical Communications Programs and Classes." *Technical Writing Teacher,* 1982, 9 (3), 137–146.

Courts, P. L., and McInerney, K. H. *Assessment in Higher Education: Politics, Pedagogy, and Portfolios.* Westport, CT: Praeger, 1993.

Frick, J. "Portfolio Assessment, English Majors, and Curriculum Development." Paper presented at the 45th annual conference on College Composition and Communication, Nashville, Tennessee, Mar. 1994.

Ganahl, D. J., and Ganahl, R. J. "Assessing Baccalaureate Advertising Outcomes Utilizing Marketing Education Curriculum Development Strategies." Paper presented at the 75th annual meeting of the Association for Education in Journalism and Mass Communication, Montreal, Quebec, Canada, Aug. 1992.

Winsor, J. L. *Establishing Professional Advisory Councils for Communication Programs.* Washington, D.C.: Office of Educational Research and Improvement, Educational Resources and Improvement Center, 1992.

Winter, J. K., and Winter, E. J. "Using the Portfolio Approach in Teaching Intercultural Business Communication." Paper presented at the 11th annual Eastern Michigan University Conference on Languages and Communication for World Business and the Professions, Ypsilanti, Mar. 1992.

W. Tracy Dillon directs the professional writing program for the Department of English and is an assessment associate in the Center for Academic Excellence, Office of Academic Affairs, at Portland State University, Portland, Oregon.

How Can We Judge the Impact and the Validity of Portfolios?

Validating Recognition and Production Measures for the Bachelor of Science in Social Work

Frank J. Spicuzza, Maryanne Lynch Cunningham

How well do portfolios measure student outcomes as compared to other conventional measures, such as grades and multiple choice tests? Faculty at the University of Tennessee, Knoxville, began to explore this very question, when they set about to test the validity of a two-tiered process in which students take a test as well as complete a portfolio. This process has been used to assess the effectiveness of curriculum in the bachelor of science in social work program. From Assessment Update 5:5, *September-October 1993.*

Assessment of the Bachelor of Science in Social Work (BSSW) at the University of Tennessee, Knoxville (UTK), has two components. The first part of the instrument is a traditional paper-and-pencil test composed of 100 multiple-choice items linked to the teaching and learning occurring in the classroom. Only items matched to the program's goals and judged important for practice are included. These recognition measures reflect general knowledge of social work defined as professional foundation. Each foundation area—human behavior and the social environment, practice methods, research, and social welfare—is represented in the multiple-choice items in proportion to the number of courses offered in the curricular area. Each question is worth one point, so the highest possible score for this part is 100 points.

The focus of the second part of the assessment process is the application of knowledge through practice. Each student submits a well-organized portfolio that provides evidence of practice competence. Course assignments, examinations, volunteer experiences, field practice activities, and field evaluations are selected by the student to exhibit skill in four basic areas: information gathering and assessment, the development and use of the professional self, practice activities with various client systems and organizations, and evaluation of professional activities. All these skill areas are considered essential for competent practice; they are not rank-ordered. Students select or reject any previous work and organize the portfolio as they wish. They articulate reasons for their choices and provide evidence of self-reflection. This procedure encourages students to take risks, create, explore, and assess self. Whereas the multiple-choice test is a single snapshot of a student's achievement, the portfolio is a purposeful reflection of a student's progress and performance over time.

Two faculty members separately review each portfolio to determine the level of accomplishment in each skill area. A list of questions is provided to the reviewers to assist them in the evaluation process. Each reviewer must cite evidence of skill attainment and determine the degree of attainment. Both reviewers assign a score based on a 100-point scale. These scores are averaged for a final rating of the portfolio.

The portfolio score is combined with the score from the multiple-choice test and averaged for a final score for the BSSW assessment. The procedure stresses content and application equally and furnishes comprehensive coverage of the program's educational outcomes.

BSSW majors are alerted to the dual-assessment method when entering the program, and the portfolio process is discussed in each of the professional courses. Faculty makes a special effort to create a climate conducive to portfolio development. Students are informed that a portfolio is not a scrapbook or unfocused collection of information but rather an organized, individualized portrait of what has been accomplished (Varvus,

1990). It is a collection of evidence reflecting the critical tasks of entry practice. To increase the incentive for students to do their best work and to ensure that all graduating seniors are tested, assessment is an integral segment of a required integrative seminar. One session of the seminar is used for the multiple-choice examination, and the portfolio is the principal course assignment.

We undertook a validation study of this dual-assessment process using several procedures. First, the scores from part I (objective questions) were correlated with the scores from part II (portfolio) of the 69 seniors who completed the assessment. The correlation between the two parts, $r = .547$, was significant ($p < .0001$). This result suggests that the scores of part I and part II go up and down together. Approximately 30% of the variation in part I scores is explained by part II scores. The positive correlation is somewhat comforting, since social work practice is guided by knowledge.

In a second test of validity, we correlated the total score (parts I and II) of the assessment with both the overall cumulative grade-point average (GPA) and cumulative grade-point average in the major (SW-GPA) of the 69 seniors. The correlations with both GPA ($r = .476$) and SW-GPA ($r = .612$) were significant ($p < .0001$). The results reinforce the validity of the two-part assessment process.

In another procedure to examine the validity of the assessment process, we related the portfolio score (part II) with three process subscale scores—communicating, solving problems, and clarifying values—of the College Outcome Measures Project (COMP) examination. The COMP exam, a test of effective adult functioning, was selected because of the number of seniors who have completed it and its emphasis on several of the skills central to social work practice. Twenty (29%) social work seniors who had completed the assessment had also taken the general education exam. The low level of senior involvement in general education assessment is due to the large number of transfer students in the baccalaureate social work program. Transfer students can waive this requirement if they have been enrolled at the university for less than 24 months.

In contrast to the strong correlations between the BSSW assessment and students' performance in coursework, as measured by cumulative grade-point averages, the association with scores on the COMP exam was quite weak. When the two measures of coursework performance (GPA and SW-GPA) and scores on the two sections of the BSSW assessment were correlated with the three process subscales of the COMP, only the relationship between part I scores (multiple-choice examination) and the clarifying values process subscale was statistically significant ($r = .506$, $p = .0228$). No other correlations were statistically significant at the $p <$ .05 level. The limited sample size may play a role in the results.

This validation study provided support for the use of the two-part BSSW assessment in gauging a student's knowledge and skills for entry practice at the time of graduation. There is evidence of concurrent validity in the relationship between part I and part II on the instrument, as well as between students' cumulative performance in coursework and the total score of the outcome measure. However, there is little evidence of a relationship with the three process subscales of the COMP exam.

The results of the validation study are not surprising. Often standardized tests, such as the COMP, are detached from teaching and learning activity in the classroom. The BSSW assessment is directly related to the education and training of baccalaureate social work students at the University of Tennessee, Knoxville. The instrument is tailored to the educational objectives of the program and grounded in the critical tasks of entry professional practice. The portfolio section of the examination allows students to exhibit and evaluate their real work and to provide a historical record within the context of their classroom and field practice experience. This performance evaluation has the potential to create an authentic composite view of what social work students have learned and are able to do.

This dual procedure provides feedback to students but is also a chance to review the curriculum and to monitor instruction. In addition, the portfolio assignment furnishes materials that can be used to display the richness and complexities of social work education to interested parties who focus on program effectiveness and fiscal responsibility.

The BSSW assessment process has a few disadvantages. Like other lo-cally developed instruments, it may be less credible externally than a stan-dardized test would be. Obviously, comparative information from other programs is not available. The other concern about this two-part assess-ment is the time it takes. Are the results worth the time and effort of ini-tial test construction and then, each year, of building a "portfolio environment," grading a paper-and-pencil test, evaluating portfolios, mon-itoring the process, and documenting the results? It is a labor-intensive process, but the results of the validity study and the potential for individ-ual and program assessment indicate that the benefits outweigh the neg-atives.

Reference

Varvus, L. "Put Portfolios to the Test." *Instructor*, 1990, *100*(1), 48–53.

Frank J. Spicuzza is associate professor in the College of Social Work, University of Tennessee, Knoxville. Maryanne Lynch Cunningham is assistant director of Research and Evaluation Services, University of Tennessee, Knoxville.

An Evaluation of Portfolio Assessment: A Student Perspective

Frank J. Spicuzza

What kind of impact do portfolios have on students? Do they alter students' perceptions of their educational experiences? Here is another article drawing on the portfolios used in the college of social work at the University of Tennessee, Knoxville, this time to ex-plore students' perceptions of portfolio assessment. From Assessment Update *8:6, November–December 1996.*

A plethora of reports and studies praise the value and the advantages of portfolio assessment (for example, Buschman, 1993; Knight and Gallaro, 1994; Paulson and Paulson, 1990; "A Conversation with Grant Wiggins,"

1990; Wolfe, 1991). Testimonials from educators focus on the growth of student learning due to portfolio assessment, but little is shared with regard to the students' perceptions of this process. Do students perceive that their professional and personal growth is enhanced by this outcomes assessment process and product? To answer this question, I initiated a dual procedure to assess the perceptions of 87 seniors in social work who each completed a portfolio as part of an examination in their major field of study prior to their graduation in 1994, 1995, or 1996.

Method

The seniors were requested to provide a self-report identifying their perceptions of this assessment process. Their written comments were to be included in the conclusions of their portfolios. The students were to indicate benefits, if any, of the portfolio in terms of understanding of self, preparation for employment or graduate school, understanding of social work, comprehension of the curriculum, enhancement of decision-making skills, and any other area of their choice. Written directions emphasized that the seniors did not have to address each identified area, but rather they were to "provide an honest self-report."

The 1994, 1995, and 1996 seniors were also invited to participate in an in-class survey designed to assess the portfolio process. Those who completed the survey were not identified. Using a 4-point Likert scale, the students were asked to rate the extent to which their involvement in the portfolio process had enhanced their personal and professional growth, understanding of the curriculum, and preparation for employment or graduate school. The completed surveys were collected by a member of the class and delivered to the department secretary. The purpose of the survey was to enhance the credibility of the information provided in the self-reports.

Self-Report Findings

Three themes were evident in the self-reports written by the 87 seniors. The seniors were consistent in their view of the portfolio as a challenging assignment, an integrating experience, and a confidence builder.

The seniors stressed that the development of a portfolio was more challenging than they had expected. One student indicated that "in the back of my mind I thought it would be a breeze, but I was so wrong." The seniors had been alerted to this assessment process upon entry to the baccalaureate social work program. In each social work class the portfolio process is addressed and students are reminded to save their assignments and tests. Thus, in most cases, the seniors had been collecting materials that reflected attainment of the program's education outcomes for more than three years. One senior lamented, "I had compiled a bushel of information." The struggle was not the collection of data, but what information to use, ultimately, and how to use it. The seniors questioned what to include in their records of achievement, and, in so doing, they made decisions about the pertinence of the items to the education outcomes or competencies as well as the quality of the work.

The students' self-reports contained consistent references to sorting and sifting through the significant number of assignments, examinations, case studies, and field practice materials to select their best work. Often, there was mention of reviewing assignments in the introductory social work courses and comparing them to the more advanced work completed in the upper-division classes. The process of gathering and examining their work enabled the seniors to reflect on their strengths and weaknesses as entry-level social workers, their changing interest in and perceptions of social work practice, and their need for continual development. Consensus emerged among the seniors that a critical examination of one's work and professional growth is a difficult, time-consuming task.

The seniors' self-reports made reference to the portfolio process as an integrating experience. In meeting the challenge of organizing and reflecting on their previous work, the seniors recognized the major themes of the curriculum as well as the mission of the program. They reported that a significant portion of their work reflected an appreciation of human diversity, the values of the profession, the problem-solving process of helping, and social systems theory. The assignments, activities, and coursework were mechanisms to assist them in acquiring the knowledge, skills, and values for entry practice. One student vividly described her apartment floor covered with assignments and tests and her sudden realization that her educational experience was spread out before her. The "carpet" of previous work was a reminder of all she had accomplished in her classes and practica in preparation for practice. The creation of a portfolio brought the numerous pieces of the curriculum together as a whole. Another student commented that "in essence, the portfolio represents the entire curriculum . . . in my own words and experiences."

The portfolios provided confirmation to the seniors that they had developed basic competencies for professional practice and additional confidence for future professional development. The seniors had concrete evidence of their abilities, which enhanced their self-esteem and their appreciation of the breadth and depth of their educational experience. The perception of confidence was pervasive throughout the self-reports. Every senior made reference to having a great sense of accomplishment and feeling more secure and well prepared for entry practice or graduate school. One senior wrote, "Indeed I feel fortunate when I look to see where I have been and confident when I look to see where I am going."

Approximately half of the students mentioned that they had not realized how much they had accomplished or the number of skills they had developed. Some students identified specific skills, such as problem-solving, assessment, case management, and writing ability, that had been further developed, while others focused more generally on their growth in empathy and understanding of people.

The portfolio process affirmed the seniors' professional identity and their strong foundation for future growth. This confidence enabled students to identify their skill deficiencies and gaps in knowledge. Students admitted that they had to develop their assessment and evaluation skills further and to learn more about certain client groups, research methodologies, and models of policy analysis. They had the confidence and strength to look at themselves and to realize they had grown. They also realized the need to continue to learn and grow. In referring to the ongoing process of development, one student indicated, "The more I think I know about people and their complex problems, the more I discover how little I really know." This type of response is generated by confidence.

Survey Findings

The 1994, 1995, and 1996 seniors were requested to complete a survey anonymously that addressed whether the portfolio process had assisted them in their personal and professional growth, skill development, and understanding of the curriculum. Overall, 59 of the 87 seniors (69%) returned the survey. Using a 4-point Likert scale (1 = not at all helpful, 2 = somewhat helpful, 3 = helpful, and 4 = extremely helpful), the seniors indicated that the portfolio was helpful in all of the identified areas. The lowest mean score for any one of the items was 2.52 (see Table 1).

The seniors were very appreciative of the portfolio in furthering their understanding of curriculum themes and the benefits of specific courses. The portfolio appeared to be an integrative process that enabled students to clearly identify themes that tied the curriculum together. Moreover, in reviewing and organizing their coursework, the seniors were able to identify specific courses that significantly influenced their personal and professional development.

The seniors were also appreciative of the portfolio process in furthering their understanding of self and their professional growth. However, they were less enthusiastic about the process as a means of facilitating their

Table 1. Student Perceptions of Portfolio Involvement

Item	Mean Scores
Understanding of curriculum themes	3.62
Appreciation of specific courses	3.48
Understanding of self	3.13
Professional growth	3.11
Appreciation of human diversity	3.00
Preparation for employment or graduate school	2.98
Decision-making skills	2.87
Writing skills	2.52

Note: N = 59; items scored on a 4-point scale ranging from 1 (not at all helpful) to 4 (extremely helpful).

skill development and preparation for employment and graduate school. This finding was surprising since the very nature of portfolio construction involves decision-making and writing skills, which are essential for employment and graduate school. The responses across the three senior classes did not differ significantly.

Student Perceptions

Based on analysis of the survey results and the comments found in the self-reports, it appears that the students felt very confident that the portfolio has been beneficial in promoting their personal and professional growth. These feelings are reflected in the consistent references to increased self-confidence and greater awareness of their accomplishments. However, the survey results indicate that the seniors felt the development of a portfolio was "somewhat helpful" to "helpful" in the further development of writing and decision-making skills and preparation for employment or graduate school. For these seniors, the portfolio appears to have had a more positive impact on self-esteem and professional growth and a more limited influence on specific skill development and preparation for the future.

The survey responses and self-reports are consistent in stressing the importance of the portfolio in understanding the curriculum and the value of specific courses. The references in the self-reports to the portfolio as "a great review" and "an integrating experience" were reinforced by the high mean scores on the survey items referring to the curriculum.

Conclusions and Observations

The literature refers to portfolios as an excellent tool to assess personal and professional growth, skill development, and instructional goals. The portfolio is discussed as an empowerment experience in that it fosters self-assessment, self-motivation, self-respect, and future growth. The positive perceptions of our social work students underscore the testimony provided by educators. Although one must remember that perceptions are often colored by a variety of personal considerations, the seniors reflect the thinking of educators who view portfolios as the strategy of choice in outcomes assessment.

Portfolio assessment is flawed, as is any type of assessment approach. Portfolios are difficult to score, not readily comparable, problematic in terms of reliability and validity, and time-consuming. Although challenges are present, no other method of assessment appears to equal portfolios in the enhancement of student empowerment and motivation. This assessment mechanism gives students control over their work and promotes self-reflection. By constructing their stories and charting their growth as learners, the members of the three senior classes in my study gained confidence as well as an understanding of where they had been, what they had done, and where they were going. The portfolio process appears to energize students (Rich, 1994).

The results of this study are not surprising. Our social work program has carefully planned the portfolio process. The portfolio is directly tailored to the program's education outcomes and grounded in the competence of entry-level professional social work practice. Batzle (1992) stressed that portfolio assessment should reflect the distinct qualities and purposes of a program. At Tennessee, students are alerted to the program's education outcomes in each social work class and the portfolio process is discussed in relation to these goals. Standards for exemplary portfolios are identified and examples of high-quality portfolios from previous classes are placed on reserve in the university library. Students are reminded that they must be able to demonstrate in the last term of their senior year that they have successfully met the program's education outcomes. Each academic and field practice course provides learning experiences that enable students to develop materials that provide a historical record of what they have learned and what they have been able to do. Students know what is expected of them, are aware of the criteria for evaluation, and have the opportunity to develop and collect appropriate data for their portfolios.

Successful portfolio development involves risk-taking and self-reflection. These behaviors will not occur unless an appropriate learning environment has been established. Throughout the curriculum, students are encouraged to make choices and to take appropriate risks in the class-room. They are required to make self-appraisals as they encounter the challenges of social work practice. As a result of this exposure, the seniors are not overwhelmed with the task of developing a portfolio.

Student motivation is a significant factor for assessment success. In the social work program, the portfolio is the major course assignment of a required integrative seminar for seniors. The portfolio is graded and is significant in the determination of the course grade. Gray (1989) warned educators that any assessment process should be part of a course grade if it is to be taken seriously by students. Alumni, who are guest speakers in the seminar, discuss the development of their portfolios and the perceived benefits of this experience. Their references to the value of the portfolio in increasing their self-confidence and assisting them in employment or graduate school help to motivate the seniors to do their best work.

Each portfolio is evaluated by two faculty members using criteria de-rived from the program's education outcomes. Both faculty members meet with the student to discuss the strengths and deficiencies of the portfolio and to provide information regarding the student's progress toward meet-ing the program's education outcomes. The meetings with program fac-ulty convey to the students not only that feedback is a constructive part of reaching goals but also that the faculty value outcomes assessment. Al-though a time-consuming process, provision of high-quality, distinct feed-back is an essential component of any type of outcomes assessment (Wiggins, 1993).

The context or setting of the portfolio process influences its success. The research reported on here focused on a program that planned very carefully the implementation of portfolio assessment and developed a port-folio environment. This program may be atypical since one study indicates that "portfolios are frequently initiated with limited planning and without a clear understanding of the varieties of purposes they may serve" (Bernick and McDonald, 1994, p. 4). In addition to this circumstance, my study was limited to the perceptions of a small number of seniors majoring in a sin-gle discipline. The findings are based on self-reports and a survey completed by three senior classes. There was no attempt to categorize the seniors by age, sex, and cumulative grade point average and to compare responses. Further research is warranted to address these limitations.

In an age of accountability, the portfolio has become a rapidly growing assessment trend in postsecondary education. Just as testimonials are insufficient to verify the value of a program or institution, they are inadequate to substantiate the worth of an assessment process. Do portfolios achieve the learning objectives claimed in testimonials by educators? The response to this question by 87 seniors who completed a portfolio as a requirement for graduation in a social work program is affirmative. Would the positive response to this procedure be present without careful planning in the educational unit? My response to this question is a resounding no.

References

Arter, J. *Portfolio Resources*. Portland, Oreg.: Northwest Regional Educational Laboratory, 1991.

Batzle, J. *Portfolio Assessment and Evaluation: Developing and Using Portfolios in the Classroom*. Cypress, Calif.: Creative Teaching Press, 1992.

Bernick, R., and McDonald, C. "Planning for Portfolio Assessment." *Assessment Alternatives Newsletter*, 1994, 4–7.

Bok, D. "Reclaiming the Public Trust." *Change*, 1992, *24* (4), 13–19.

Buschman, L. "Alternative Assessment: Students and Teachers Doing Assessment Together." *Assessment Alternatives Newsletter*, 1993, 5–10.

"A Conversation with Grant Wiggins." *Instructor*, 1990, *100* (1), 51.

Forrest, A. *Time Will Tell: Portfolio-Assisted Assessment of General Education*. Washington, D.C.: American Association for Higher Education, 1990.

Gray, P. *Assessment Update*, 1989, *1* (2), 4–5.

Knight, M., and Gallaro, D. (eds.). *Portfolio Assessment: Applications of Portfolio Analysis*. Lanham, Md.: University Press of America, 1994.

Meyer, C., Schuman, S., and Angello, N. *Northwestern Evaluation Association White Paper on Aggregating Portfolio Data*. Lake Oswego, Oreg.: Northwest Evaluation Association, 1990.

Ohlhausen, M., and Ford, M. "Portfolio Assessment in Teacher Education: A Tale of Two Cities." Paper presented at the annual meeting of the National Reading Conference, Miami, Fla., 1990.

Paulson, F., and Paulson, P. "How Do Portfolios Measure Up? A Cognitive Model for Assessing Portfolios." Paper presented at the annual meeting of the Northwest Evaluation Association, Union, Wash., 1990.

Rich, S. "Test Me, Test Me Not: The Portfolio Alternative for Developmental Writers." In M. Knight and D. Gallaro (eds.), *Portfolio Assessment: Applications of Portfolio Analysis.* Lanham, Md.: University Press of America, 1994.

Vavrus, L. "Put Portfolios to the Test." *Instructor,* 1990, *100* (1), 48–53.

White, M. "Portfolios as an Assessment Concept." In L. Black and others (eds.), *New Directions in Portfolio Assessment: Reflective Practice, Critical Theory, and Large-Scale Scoring.* Portsmouth, N.H.: Boynton-Cook, 1994.

Wiggins, G. "Assessment: Authenticity, Context, and Validity." *Phi Delta Kappan,* 1993, *75* (3), 200–214.

Wolf, K. "The Schoolteacher's Portfolio: Issues in Design, Implementation, and Evaluation." *Phi Delta Kappan,* 1991, *73* (2), 129–136.

Wolfe, B. "The New Assessments: Talking the Talk and Walking the Walk." *Portfolio Assessment Newsletter,* 1991, *3* (1), 1–2.

Frank J. Spicuzza is associate professor in the College of Social Work at the University of Tennessee, Knoxville. Preparation of this manuscript was made possible, in part, by a grant from the University of Tennessee, Knoxville, Professional Development Awards Program.

A Change in Culture: Pepperdine University's CD-ROM Student Portfolio Project

Don Thompson, Cynthia Cornell Novak

Portfolios can provide rich feedback to both students and faculty. How can this feedback be put to good use? How can institutions make sure that valuable information doesn't get lost? This article describes how Pepperdine University faculty used portfolios to create a culture of improvement. From Assessment Update 9:5, September-October 1997.

It is 2:40 A.M. on the Pepperdine University campus in Malibu, California. Sara, a student majoring in sports medicine, answers one final question on the spring assessment interview posed by the assessment director.

Satisfied with her answer, she hits the enter key and concludes the interview.

Hundreds of students in colleges and universities around the country are working to help faculty and administrators compile assessment data on the programs at their schools. What makes Sara and the other 43 students in the Pepperdine University CD-ROM Student Portfolio Project unique is that the information they generate is stored and navigated via the World Wide Web. Thus, the project participants can fulfill their responsibilities as assessment project participants at their convenience (at 2:40 A.M.?), and the assessment team, composed of faculty and administrators, can access the data at their convenience (at 2:40 P.M.?).

The CD-ROM Student Portfolio Project is a four-year longitudinal study that began in the fall of 1994 under the direction of Don Thompson, a professor of mathematics and Great Books, and Lee Carroll, a professor of English and director of the Freshman Writing Program. The project began with 80 randomly selected first-year seminar students. The 44 students who have participated for the duration of the project consist of two cohort groups from the incoming classes of 1994 and 1995. The overall group consists of 28 women and 16 men.

The Portfolio Project focuses on analysis of empirical evidence of student learning and college experience. Student participants provide the data by submitting their course syllabi, tests, quizzes, papers, projects, videotaped speeches, and portfolios. In addition, they engage in audiotaped in-depth interviews and videotaped focus groups each semester as well as periodic on-line self-assessments. All materials are digitized and stored on a Silicon Graphics computer and then organized into individual student Web pages. At the end of four years, as participants prepare for graduation, their materials are recorded on CD-ROM disks, which they can use as they search for jobs. Their materials will be maintained on individual Web pages for five years after their graduation.

Faculty Assessment Seminars

The World Wide Web affords faculty assessment teams the opportunity to access and examine student work from their offices. Furthermore, because large quantities of data can be navigated efficiently, faculty members are able to make comparisons among student work and make assessment decisions on-line.

During the summers of 1995 and 1996, faculty members representing the disciplines of literature, social science, fine arts, composition, communications, Asian studies, teacher education, and natural science met for several weeks to look closely at assessment issues and, in particular, at the CD-ROM Portfolio Project data. Faculty members were interested in answering the following question from *Strong Foundations* (Association of American Colleges, 1994): How do strong general education programs embody institutional mission? To answer the question, the faculty focused on the following part of the university mission statement: "All graduates will have the ability to think clearly, logically, independently, and critically." The faculty were interested in determining how critical, logical, independent thinking was evidenced in student work across the general education program.

Since faculty members in the seminar represented a diversity of disciplines, the first challenge was to define critical thinking and reasoning. They decided to use as one method of analysis Bloom's (1956) Taxonomy of Educational Objectives, both the cognitive and affective categories. Faculty members examined each student's semester of work, looking systematically at it through the lens of Bloom's cognitive categories (for example, knowledge through evaluation) and affective categories (for example, receiving through holding a value or complex of values).

The faculty assessment team looked at each of the following elements of coursework and answered questions as they evaluated the degree to which a course addressed critical thinking and reasoning:

Syllabus: Is there language in the syllabus reflecting critical thinking goals? How will the goals be demonstrated in the course?

Assignments: What kind of critical thinking is asked for by the professor in written form (for example, assigned papers, tests, quizzes, homework, reports, and lab).

Instructor feedback: What kind of evidence of critical thinking goals exists in the professor's grading of the work? Does the professor model a need for critical thinking in his or her responses to the student?

Portfolio: What evidence of critical thinking and reasoning is there in written form in the student's portfolio of work? What are the behavioral measures that this student has been challenged with to think critically during the semester?

Student feedback: Is there any evidence that the student has been asked to do self-evaluation about the skills being acquired or about the ways in which the assignments are evaluated?

Self-assessment (for example, audiotaped interview and on-line self assessment): In the student's semester-end academic self-assessment, what evidence is there of reflection on the critical thinking value-addedness of this course? Is there any mention of critical thinking enhancement during the tape-recorded interviews?

As we worked with these six categories, a hexagonal model emerged. We noticed that the first three categories involve the instructor's perspective of student learning while the last three stress student perceptions. This assessment model affords a single image whereby those assessing a course can tell at a glance the degree to which critical thinking has been demanded and the degree to which a student has been able to respond.

Faculty evaluators ranked each category qualitatively with a number between 0 (no critical thinking evident) and 10 (high critical thinking evident), generating an image that captured both professor and student effectiveness in critical thinking and reasoning. Interrater reliability for these rankings was achieved through a process of individual analysis, written reports, and group discussion.

Outcomes

At the conclusion of the seminars, faculty generated the following list of recommendations based on their close study of the CD-ROM Portfolio Project data: First, the general education program needs a director, someone who can stand above the process and see how and where connections should be made. Second, teacher evaluations should be examined since in this consumer culture students who are asked whether they like a course may respond negatively even though the course may have challenged them to think critically. Third, class size should be examined, especially the large lecture formats used for general education courses such as Western Heritage and Religion. Fourth, faculty loads should be examined so that faculty have time to develop courses that stress critical thinking or interdisciplinary approaches. Fifth, a mandate needs to come from the faculty to overhaul the twelve-year-old general education program.

Some progress has been made. The dean appointed a director of general education and assessment; however, the position only releases the faculty member for one course each semester (fall, winter, and spring). Faculty loads also have been modified such that full-time, tenure-track faculty teach three courses each of two terms, with the summers off for research and writing.

Although this progress is heartening, more needs to be done by way of continuing to strengthen the faculty culture of assessment so that eventually the faculty themselves call for a mandate to redesign the general education curriculum. Despite the work that lies ahead, conversations about assessment are more frequent and more honest among once-fragmented faculty constituencies. More information about this project can be found at our Web address: <http://cdrpp.pepperdine.edu>.

References

Association of American Colleges. *Strong Foundations: 12 Principles for Effective General Education Programs*. Washington, D.C.: Association of American Colleges, 1994.

Bloom, B. S. (ed.). *Taxonomy of Educational Objectives: The Classification of Educational Goals*. New York: Longman, Green, 1956.

Don Thompson is dean of academic programs and professor of mathematics and Great Books at Pepperdine University, Malibu, California. He can be reached at <thompson@pepperdine.edu>. Cynthia Cornell Novak is associate professor of humanities and director of the Freshman Writing Program at Pepperdine University. She can be reached at <cnovak@pepperdine.edu>.